Sushi

Bath · New York · Singapore · Hong Kong · Cologne · Delhi · Melbourne

This edition published in 2009

Parragon Publishing
Queen Street House
4 Queen Street
Bath BA1 1HE, UK

ISBN 978-1-4075-4950-7

Printed in China

Notes for the Reader

This book uses imperial, metric, and US cup measurements. Follow the same units of measurement throughout; do not mix imperial and metric. All spoon measurements are level: teaspoons are assumed to be 5 ml, and tablespoons are assumed to be 15 ml. Unless otherwise stated, milk is assumed to be whole, eggs and individual vegetables, such as potatoes, are medium, and pepper is freshly ground black pepper.

The times given are an approximate guide only. Preparation times differ according to the techniques used by different people and the cooking times may also vary from those given as a result of the type of oven used. Optional ingredients, variations, or serving suggestions have not been included in the calculations.

Recipes using raw or very lightly cooked eggs should be avoided by infants, the elderly, pregnant women, convalescents, and anyone with a chronic condition. Pregnant and breastfeeding women are advised to avoid eating peanuts and peanut products. People with nut allergies should be aware that some of the prepared ingredients used in the recipes in this book may contain nuts. Always check the package before use.

Picture acknowledgment
The publisher would like to thank Getty Images for permission to reproduce copyright material for the front cover.

Sushi

introduction

Sushi is so much more than just raw fish and rice. Though the word sushi means simply vinegared rice, this elegant and stylish form of Japanese cookery is immensely varied and versatile. You can make sushi with cooked fish, meat, eggs, cheese, and all manner of vegetables. So long as your ingredients go well with the rice—and most foods do—then you can make wonderful sushi.

Sushi masters train for years, but don't let that deter you. Making simple sushi is a lot easier than it looks. Some of the basic techniques require a little practice, but you will soon get the hang of them. You don't need a lot of specialist equipment in order to make great sushi, but you will probably find the art of sushi more satisfying if you invest

in a few tools: a sushi press, a rice spatula, and perhaps a bamboo bowl for mixing the rice in. However, the only essential is a sushi rolling mat.

As you learn to make sushi you will encounter new ways of preparing and

serving food as well as some strange and unusual ingredients. It's very important that all the elements of the meal are absolutely fresh, that the flavors are clean, and that they look good on the plate. Japanese food is meant to please the eye as well as the palate.

Sushi is also fantastically healthy. It is low in fat and packed with nutrients—seaweed, for example, is rich in vitamins and minerals, oily fish such as mackerel is a good source of useful fatty acids. Wasabi (Japanese horseradish) and rice vinegar aid the digestion.

Sushi is traditionally made with raw fish, which must be absolutely fresh. Source your fish from a reputable supplier who sells 'sashimi-

grade' fish, intended for serving raw. Take your fish straight home, preferably in a cool-bag with fresh ice, put into the refrigerator, and use it on the day that you buy it. Prepare your fish at the last moment, and eat your sushi soon after preparing it.

sushi
rolls

Sushi rolls (*maki zushi*) look really impressive, but they are one of the easiest types of sushi to make at home. The only special equipment that you need is a sushi rolling mat. These bamboo mats are inexpensive, and they are widely available from good kitchen stores—even some supermarkets.

Sushi rolls are made up of sheets of nori (seaweed) spread with vinegared rice and various tasty fillings. You then roll the sheets into a tube and cut them into bite-sized pieces. They are served cut-side up so that you can see the filling inside, and you should eat them within an hour or two of making them.

Sushi rolls can be thin, with just one or two fillings, or quite thick, with up to five or six. Thin rolls are easier to make, so it is best to start off with these. The main thing to remember is to keep the filling evenly spread, and not to use so much that the wrapping splits. Don't worry if your filling falls out of the ends when you are rolling; you can just push it back in, or trim the ends before cutting the roll.

Always use a wet knife and wipe it on a damp cloth between each cut. Keep a bowl of water to which you have added a splash of rice vinegar to hand so that you can dampen your hands before handling the sticky rice.

perfect sushi rice

ingredients

**MAKES 22 OZ/
625 G/4 CUPS**

10 oz/300 g/scant 1¼ cups
    sushi rice

12 fl oz/350 ml/scant
    1½ cups water

2-inch/5-cm square piece of
    kombu (sun-dried kelp,
    optional)

2 tbsp sushi rice seasoning
    (or 2 tbsp rice vinegar,
    1 tbsp sugar, and ¼ tsp
    salt combined)

method

1 Place the rice in a strainer and rinse under cold water until the water runs completely clear. Drain the rice, then place in a pan with the water.

2 Cut a few slits in the kombu, if using, to help release the flavor, then add to the rice. Cover the pan with a tight-fitting lid and bring to a boil. Remove the kombu and quickly replace the lid. Reduce the heat and let simmer for 10 minutes. Remove from the heat and let stand for 15 minutes. Do not lift the lid to take a look once you have removed the kombu.

3 Turn the cooked rice into a large, flat-bottomed, nonmetallic bowl. Pour the rice seasoning evenly over the surface of the rice, then use quick cutting strokes to mix it in with a spatula. Do not stir or you will break the rice grains. As you work, fan the rice with either a hand-held fan or an electric one set to the lowest setting.

4 Keep slicing and fanning until the rice has reached room temperature and looks shiny. Cover with a damp cloth and use the same day; do not refrigerate.

classic tuna nori rolls

ingredients

MAKES 24 PIECES

2 sheets of toasted nori
½ quantity freshly cooked
    sushi rice (see page 8)
wasabi paste
2 oz/55 g sashimi-grade
    tuna, cut into strips
    ¼ inch/5 mm square
Japanese soy sauce and
    pickled ginger, to serve

method

1 Fold a nori sheet in half lengthwise, press all along the fold, and tear it into 2 equal pieces. Place a half-sheet smooth-side down on a sushi rolling mat so that one of the long edges is directly in front of you.

2 Divide the rice into 4 equal portions. Wet your hands, then spread 1 portion of rice evenly over the nori, leaving a ½-inch/1-cm clear border along the furthest edge.

3 Dab a thin line of wasabi paste across the rice at the end nearest you. Cover with a quarter of the tuna strips, arranged in a continuous line.

4 Pick up the nearest edge of the rolling mat. Slowly roll the mat away from you to wrap the nori around the filling. Use gentle, even pressure and lift the mat out of the way as you go. Press the roll onto the uncovered border of the nori to seal it.

5 Transfer the roll to a chopping board, seam-side down. Cut it in half and then cut each half into 3 equal pieces using a wet, very sharp knife. Wipe your knife between each cut. Repeat to make 3 more rolls. Serve with soy sauce, pickled ginger, and extra wasabi.

salmon & arugula rolls with pesto

ingredients

MAKES 24 PIECES

2 sheets of toasted nori
½ quantity freshly cooked
    sushi rice (see page 8)
pesto
2 oz/55 g skinless sashimi-
    grade fillet of salmon,
    cut into strips
    ½ inch/1 cm square
1½ oz/40 g arugula, stalks
    removed
Japanese soy sauce, pickled
    ginger, and wasabi paste,
    to serve

method

1 Fold a nori sheet in half lengthwise, press all along the fold, and tear it into 2 equal pieces. Place a half-sheet smooth-side down on a sushi rolling mat so that one of the long edges is directly in front of you.

2 Divide the rice into 4 equal portions. Using wet hands, spread 1 portion of the rice evenly over the nori, leaving a ½-inch/1-cm clear border along the furthest edge.

3 Dab a thin line of pesto across the rice at the end nearest you. Cover with a quarter of the salmon strips, arranging them in a continuous line, and top with arugula.

4 Pick up the nearest edge of the rolling mat. Slowly roll the mat away from you to wrap the nori around the filling. Use gentle, even pressure and lift the mat out of the way as you go. Press the roll onto the uncovered border of the nori to seal it.

5 Transfer the roll to a chopping board, seam-side down. Cut it in half and then cut each half into 3 equal pieces using a wet, very sharp knife. Repeat to make 3 more rolls. Arrange on a plate, and serve with soy sauce, pickled ginger, and wasabi paste.

tuna sesame blocks

ingredients

MAKES 12 PIECES

3¼ x 2½-inch/8 x 6-cm
   piece of tuna fillet, about
   ¾ inch/2 cm thick

2 tsp sesame oil

2 tbsp white sesame seeds,
   toasted

3 sheets of toasted nori, each
   cut into 4 strips lengthwise

2 tbsp vegetable oil

method

1 Cut the tuna into 12 cubes and roll the cubes first in the sesame oil and then in the toasted sesame seeds.

2 Roll each sesame-covered cube in a strip of nori, trimming off any excess so that the nori goes round the tuna once with little overlap.

3 Heat the vegetable oil in a skillet and put the cubes into the pan, standing them up on one nori-free end. Cook for 2 minutes, then turn over to cook the other nori-free end. The sesame seeds should be a dark brown, but not burned, and the tuna should have cooked most of the way through, leaving a rare patch in the center. If you prefer your tuna fully cooked, cook each end for a little longer.

salmon, spinach & wasabi mash rolls

ingredients

MAKES 24 PIECES

2 large starchy potatoes,
    peeled and cut into
    quarters
salt
1 scallion, finely chopped
wasabi paste
4 oz/115 g sashimi-grade
    salmon, or piece of
    salmon fillet, skin removed
1 tbsp vegetable oil (if using
    salmon fillet)
6 sheets of toasted nori
handful of baby spinach
    greens, stalks removed

method

1 Cook the potatoes in a pan of boiling salted water for 20–30 minutes, until tender. Mash, then mix with the scallion and wasabi to taste. Season with salt. Let cool, then refrigerate for 30 minutes or until very firm.

2 If using sashimi-grade salmon, cut into strips. If cooking the fish, remove any bones. Heat the oil in a skillet, then cook the salmon over medium heat for 4 minutes on each side, until cooked through. Let cool. Cut into strips.

3 Place a sheet of nori smooth-side down on a rolling mat with one of the long ends in front of you. Spread a sixth of the mashed potatoes over the bottom third of the nori. Lay a sixth of the spinach greens on top, then add a layer of salmon strips.

4 Pick up the nearest edge of the rolling mat. Slowly roll the mat away from you to wrap the nori around the filling, using gentle, even pressure. Press the roll onto the uncovered border of the nori to seal it.

5 Transfer the roll to a chopping board, seam-side down. Cut into 4 even-size pieces with a wet, very sharp knife. Repeat with the remaining ingredients.

soba noodle rolls

ingredients

MAKES 24 PIECES

4 oz/115 g sashimi-grade
   tuna or piece of tuna fillet
1 tbsp vegetable oil (if using
   tuna fillet)
3½ oz/100 g soba noodles,
   broken into pieces
1 scallion, green part only,
   thinly sliced
1 tbsp light soy sauce
½ tbsp rice wine vinegar
wasabi paste
1 tbsp finely chopped
   pickled ginger
6 sheets of toasted nori
½ English cucumber, peeled
   and finely shredded,
   seeds removed
Japanese soy sauce and
   pickled ginger, to serve

method

1 If using sashimi-grade tuna, cut into strips. If cooking the fish, heat the oil in a skillet. Sear the tuna for 30–60 seconds on all sides, so that the edges are sealed but the fish is rare in the middle. Let cool, then cut into strips.

2 Cook the soba noodles in a pan of boiling water until they are just cooked through, drain, and rinse under cold running water. Drain thoroughly. Gently mix the soba noodles with the scallion, soy sauce, rice wine vinegar, a pinch of wasabi, and the pickled ginger.

3 Put a sheet of nori smooth-side down on a rolling mat with one of the long ends in front of you. Spread a sixth of the noodle mixture over the bottom third of the nori. Lay a line of cucumber across the center of the noodles, then add a layer of tuna strips.

4 Pick up the nearest edge of the rolling mat. Slowly roll the mat away from you to wrap the nori around the filling. Use gentle, even pressure until you have finished the roll, and lift the mat out of the way as you go.

5 Transfer the roll to a chopping board, seam-side down. Cut it into 4 even-size pieces with a wet, very sharp knife. Repeat with the remaining ingredients. Serve with soy sauce, pickled ginger, and extra wasabi paste.

seven-spiced salmon rolls

ingredients

MAKES 24 PIECES

5½-oz/150-g piece of salmon
　　fillet, skin removed
sichimi togarashi (seven-spice
　　powder)
red pepper flakes
1 tbsp vegetable oil
1 quantity freshly cooked
　　sushi rice (see page 8)
6 sheets of toasted nori
2 tbsp Japanese mayonnaise
Japanese soy sauce, wasabi
　　paste, and pickled ginger,
　　to serve

method

1 Remove any bones from the salmon fillet. Dust the surface heavily with sichimi togarashi and sprinkle over a few red pepper flakes. Heat the oil in a skillet and cook the salmon over medium heat for 4 minutes on each side, or until cooked through. Let cool, then flake into large pieces.

2 Divide the rice into 6 equal portions. Put a sheet of nori smooth-side down on a rolling mat with one of the long ends toward you. With wet hands, spread 1 portion of the rice evenly over the nori, leaving a ½-inch/1-cm clear border along the furthest edge.

3 Spread 1 tsp of the mayonnaise across the the rice at the end nearest you. Lay a sixth of the flaked salmon on top of the mayonnaise.

4 Pick up the nearest edge of the rolling mat. Slowly roll the mat away from you to wrap the nori around the filling. Use gentle, even pressure and lift the mat out of the way as you go. Press the roll onto the uncovered border of the nori to seal it.

5 Transfer the roll to a chopping board, seam-side down. Cut it into 4 equal pieces with a wet, very sharp knife. Repeat with the remaining ingredients. Serve with soy sauce, wasabi, and pickled ginger.

salmon, asparagus & mayonnaise rolls

ingredients

MAKES 24 PIECES

6 thin asparagus spears

5½ oz/150 g sashimi-grade salmon, or piece of salmon fillet, skin and any bones removed

1 tbsp vegetable oil (if using salmon fillet)

6 sheets of toasted nori

1 quantity freshly cooked sushi rice (see page 8)

wasabi paste

1 tbsp Japanese mayonnaise

1 tbsp white sesame seeds, toasted

Japanese soy sauce and pickled ginger, to serve

method

1 Lay the asparagus spears flat in a skillet filled with simmering water and cook for 3–4 minutes or until tender. Cut into 3½-inch/ 9-cm lengths and let cool.

2 If using raw salmon, cut it into thin strips. If cooking the fish, heat the oil in a skillet and cook over medium heat for 4 minutes on each side, or until cooked. Let cool, then flake.

3 Put a sheet of nori smooth-side down on a rolling mat so that one of the long ends is in front of you. With wet hands, spread a sixth of the rice over the nori, leaving a ½-inch/1- cm clear border along the furthest edge.

4 Dab a line of wasabi across the rice at the end nearest you. Cover with ½ tsp of mayonnaise. Lay a cooked asparagus spear over the top and place a sixth of the salmon alongside. Sprinkle the filling with ½ tsp of the sesame seeds.

5 Pick up the nearest edge of the mat. Roll it away from you to wrap the nori around the filling, using even pressure. Press the roll onto the clear border of nori to seal it, then transfer to a chopping board. Cut it into 4 even-size pieces using a wet, very sharp knife. Repeat with the rest of the ingredients. Serve with soy sauce, pickled ginger, and more wasabi.

steamed shrimp rolls with lime dipping sauce

ingredients

MAKES 24 PIECES

14 oz/400 g/2¼ cups peeled raw shrimp, deveined

2 tbsp chopped fresh cilantro

1 large kaffir lime leaf, finely shredded

1 tbsp freshly squeezed lime juice

2 tsp sweet chili sauce

1½ tbsp fish sauce

2 tsp mirin

1 egg white

4 sheets of toasted nori

lime slices, to garnish

lime dipping sauce

4 tbsp sake

4 tbsp Japanese soy sauce

2 tsp mirin

1 tbsp freshly squeezed lime juice

method

1 Put the ingredients for the dipping sauce into a small bowl and stir to mix.

2 Place the shrimp in a blender or food processor with the chopped cilantro, shredded lime leaf, lime juice, sweet chili sauce, fish sauce, and mirin. Blend until smooth, then add the egg white and blend briefly to mix.

3 Lay a nori sheet smooth-side down on a rolling mat so that one of the short sides is in front of you. Spread a quarter of the shrimp mixture over the nori, leaving a ½-inch/1-cm clear border along the furthest edge.

4 Pick up the nearest edge of the mat. Roll the mat away from you to wrap the nori tightly around the filling, creating a pinwheel effect. Use gentle, even pressure, lifting the mat out of the way as you go. Press the roll onto the clear border to seal it. Repeat to make 3 more rolls. Place them in the refrigerator for 1 hour.

5 Transfer each roll to a chopping board, seam-side down. Cut it in half and then cut each half into 3 equal pieces using a wet, very sharp knife. Place in a steamer and cook over boiling water for 5 minutes or until the shrimp mixture is cooked. Arrange on serving plates, garnished with lime slices, with the lime dipping sauce alongside.

california rolls

ingredients

MAKES 24 PIECES

1 quantity freshly cooked
   sushi rice (see page 8)
6 sheets of toasted nori
wasabi paste
½ ripe avocado, pitted,
   peeled, and cut into thin
   strips
6 crab sticks, split in half
   lengthwise
2-inch/5-cm piece of English
   cucumber, peeled and
   cut into thin sticks
Japanese soy sauce and
   pickled ginger, to serve

method

1 Divide the rice into 6 equal portions. Place a sheet of nori smooth-side down on a rolling mat so that one of the longest ends is directly in front of you. Wet your hands and then spread 1 portion of the rice evenly over the nori, leaving a ½-inch/1-cm clear border along the furthest edge.

2 Dab a small amount of wasabi across the rice at the end nearest you. Lay a line of avocado strips on top of the wasabi, then put 2 pieces of crab stick next to them. Add a line of cucumber sticks.

3 Pick up the nearest edge of the rolling mat. Slowly roll the mat away from you to wrap the nori around the filling. Use gentle, even pressure and lift the mat out of the way as you go. Press the roll onto the uncovered border of the nori to seal it.

4 Transfer the roll to a chopping board, seam-side down. Cut it into 4 even-size pieces using a wet, very sharp knife. Repeat with the remaining ingredients. Serve with soy sauce, pickled ginger, and more wasabi.

pepper-wrapped shrimp rolls

ingredients

MAKES 12 PIECES

2 red bell peppers

1 small ripe avocado, pitted,
    peeled, and cut into slices

8 large cooked shelled shrimp

salt and black pepper

method

1 Preheat the oven to 400°F/200°C. Put the bell peppers in a roasting pan and cook them for 30 minutes, or until the skins have browned and started to puff away from the flesh. Let cool, then pull off the skins. Cut each bell pepper in half and discard the stalk, seeds, and membrane.

2 Lay out each bell-pepper half on a chopping board and place a pile of avocado slices on one side. Top with 2 shrimp and season well with salt and pepper. Roll up the bell peppers tightly, wrap each roll in plastic wrap, and let chill for 30 minutes.

3 Carefully unwrap the plastic wrap from the bell peppers and trim each end to make it straight. Cut each roll into 3 pieces with a wet, very sharp knife. Turn the pieces on their ends and arrange them on a plate.

inside-out california rolls

ingredients

MAKES 24 PIECES

1 quantity freshly cooked
sushi rice (see page 8)

6 sheets of toasted nori

¼ ripe avocado, pitted,
peeled, and cut into strips

6 crab sticks, split in half
lengthwise

2-inch/5-cm piece of English
cucumber, peeled and cut
into thin sticks

3 tbsp white sesame seeds,
toasted

Japanese soy sauce, pickled
ginger, and wasabi paste,
to serve

method

1 Divide the rice into 6 equal portions. Put a sheet of nori smooth-side down on the mat so that one of the long edges is directly in front of you. Using wet hands, spread 1 portion of the rice evenly over the nori, leaving no gaps. Lay a sheet of plastic wrap over the rice, then turn the whole thing over so that the plastic wrap is under the rice and the seaweed side is facing upwards.

2 Arrange some avocado across the nori at the end nearest you. Lay 2 pieces of crab stick next to the avocado and then add a line of thin cucumber sticks.

3 Pick up the nearest edge of the rolling mat. Slowly roll the mat away from you to wrap the rice-covered nori around the filling. Use even pressure and lift the mat out of the way as you go.

4 Spread the toasted sesame seeds over a large plate and roll the sushi in them to coat the rice evenly.

5 Transfer the roll to a chopping board, seam-side down, and cut it into 4 equal pieces with a wet, very sharp knife. Repeat with the remaining ingredients. Serve with soy sauce, pickled ginger, and wasabi.

scallop, potato & sesame rolls

ingredients

MAKES 12 PIECES

2 large starchy potatoes,
    peeled and cut into
    quarters
salt and black pepper
2 tbsp butter
1 tbsp olive oil
8 large scallops, without
    corals, cleaned
6 sheets of toasted nori
2 tbsp Japanese mayonnaise
2 tbsp white sesame seeds,
    toasted

method

1 Cook the potatoes in a pan of boiling salted water for 20–30 minutes, until tender. Mash with the butter and season with salt and pepper. Refrigerate for 30 minutes, until the mashed potatoes are very firm.

2 Heat the oil in a skillet and sauté the scallops for 2–3 minutes on each side, until cooked through. Slice them thinly into 3 coin-shaped pieces and season with salt to taste.

3 Place a sheet of nori smooth-side down on a rolling mat so that one of the long ends is toward you. Spread the mashed potatoes over the bottom third of the nori. Spread 1 tsp of mayonnaise over the top, then sprinkle on 1 tsp of the toasted sesame seeds. Add a sixth of the scallop slices.

4 Pick up the nearest edge of the rolling mat. Slowly roll the mat away from you to wrap the nori around the filling. Use gentle, even pressure until you have finished the roll, and lift the mat out of the way as you go.

5 Transfer the roll seam-side down to a chopping board and cut it into 4 even-size pieces using a wet, very sharp knife. Repeat with the remaining ingredients.

crab, asparagus & shiitake rolls

ingredients

MAKES 24 PIECES

6 thin asparagus spears
1 tbsp vegetable oil
6 fresh shiitake mushrooms,
    stalks discarded, then
    thinly sliced
6 sheets of toasted nori
1 quantity freshly cooked
    sushi rice (see page 8)
wasabi paste
6 crab sticks, split in half
    lengthwise
ponzu dipping sauce (see
    page 228), to serve

method

1 Lay the asparagus spears flat in a skillet filled with simmering water and cook for 3 minutes or until tender. Cut the spears into $3^{1}/_{2}$-inch/9-cm lengths and let cool.

2 Heat the oil in a skillet, add the mushrooms, and cook over medium heat for 5 minutes, or until softened.

3 Place a sheet of nori smooth-side down on a rolling mat so that one of the long ends is toward you. With wet hands, spread a sixth of the rice over the nori, leaving a $^{1}/_{2}$-inch/1-cm clear border along the furthest edge.

4 Dab a line of wasabi across the rice at the end nearest to you. Lay some of the cooked asparagus lengths on top of the wasabi, then put 2 pieces of crab stick next to it. Add a line of sliced mushrooms.

5 Pick up the nearest edge of the rolling mat. Roll the mat away from you to wrap the nori around the filling, using gentle, even pressure. Press the roll onto the clear border of nori to seal it. Remove the roll from the mat and cut it into 4 even-size pieces with a wet, very sharp knife. Repeat with the remaining ingredients. Serve with the ponzu dipping sauce.

shrimp & avocado skewers

ingredients

MAKES 6 SKEWERS

1 quantity freshly cooked
   sushi rice (see page 8)
6 sheets of toasted nori
1 tbsp Japanese mayonnaise
1 tsp lemon zest
12 cooked jumbo shrimp,
   shelled and deveined
2 ripe avocados, pitted,
   peeled, and cut into strips
2-inch/5-cm piece of
   cucumber, peeled and cut
   into thin sticks
pickled ginger and wasabi
   paste, to serve

method

1 Divide the rice into 6 equal portions. Put a sheet of nori smooth-side down on a rolling mat with one of the long ends toward you. Wet your hands, then spread 1 portion of the rice evenly over the nori, leaving a $1/2$-inch/1-cm clear border along the furthest edge.

2 Mix the mayonnaise with the lemon zest and spread about $1/2$ tsp in a line across the rice at the end nearest to you. Lay 2 shrimp end to end on top of the mayonnaise. Place a line of avocado next to the shrimp and then add a line of cucumber sticks.

3 Pick up the nearest edge of the rolling mat. Slowly roll the mat away from you to wrap the nori around the filling. Use gentle, even pressure and lift the mat out of the way as you go. Press the roll onto the uncovered border of the nori to seal it.

4 Transfer the roll to a chopping board, seam-side down. Cut into 4 even-size pieces with a wet, very sharp knife. Lay the pieces on their side and push a bamboo skewer through them. Repeat with the remaining ingredients to make 6 skewers in total. Serve with pickled ginger and wasabi paste.

chicken teriyaki rolls

ingredients

MAKES 24 PIECES

1 skinless, boneless chicken breast, weighing about 5½ oz/150 g, cut into strips

2 tbsp teriyaki sauce (see page 180 or use ready-made sauce)

1 tbsp vegetable oil

1 quantity freshly cooked sushi rice (see page 8)

6 sheets of toasted nori

2-inch/5-cm piece of English cucumber, peeled and cut into thin sticks

Japanese soy sauce, wasabi paste, and pickled ginger, to serve

method

1 Preheat the broiler to its highest setting. Toss the chicken in the teriyaki sauce, then the oil, and lay out on a foil-lined broiler pan. Broil the chicken strips for 4 minutes on each side, put into a bowl with any cooking juices, and let cool.

2 Divide the rice into 6 equal portions. Place a sheet of nori smooth-side down on a rolling mat so that one of the longest ends is directly in front of you. Wet your hands, then spread 1 portion of the rice evenly over the nori, leaving a ½-inch/1-cm clear border along the furthest edge.

3 Lay some of the chicken strips across the rice at the end nearest to you. Place a line of thin cucumber sticks alongside.

4 Pick up the nearest edge of the rolling mat. Slowly roll the mat away from you to wrap the nori around the filling. Use gentle, even pressure and lift the mat out of the way as you go. Press the roll onto the uncovered border of the nori to seal it.

5 Transfer the roll to a chopping board and cut it into 4 even-size pieces with a wet, very sharp knife. Repeat with the remaining ingredients. Serve with soy sauce, wasabi, and pickled ginger.

pork tonkatsu rolls

ingredients

MAKES 24 PIECES

2 tbsp flour

1 egg, lightly beaten

4 tbsp tonkatsu crumbs or
   dried white bread crumbs

7 oz/200 g pork fillet, cut into
   ¼-inch/5-mm thick slices

4 tbsp vegetable oil

1 quantity freshly cooked
   sushi rice (see page 8)

6 sheets of toasted nori

2 tbsp Japanese mayonnaise

Japanese soy sauce, pickled
   ginger, and wasabi paste,
   to serve

method

1 Put the flour, egg, and crumbs in separate bowls. One by one, dust each piece of pork in the flour, dip it in the egg, then finally press it into the crumbs. Lay the breaded pork on a plate and refrigerate for 20 minutes.

2 Heat the oil in a skillet. Add the pork and cook over medium heat for 3 minutes on each side, or until the crumbs are golden brown and the pork is cooked through. Cut the cooked slices into thin strips.

3 Divide the rice into 6 equal portions. Put a sheet of nori smooth-side down on a rolling mat so that one of the long ends is toward you. With wet hands, spread 1 portion of the rice evenly over the nori, leaving a ½-inch/1-cm clear border along the furthest edge.

4 Spread 1 tsp of the mayonnaise across the rice at the end nearest to you. Lay a sixth of the pork strips on top.

5 Pick up the nearest edge of the rolling mat. Roll the mat away from you to wrap the nori around the filling. Use gentle, even pressure and lift the mat out of the way as you go. Press the roll onto the clear border to seal it.

6 Transfer the roll to a chopping board and cut it into 4 equal pieces with a wet, very sharp knife. Repeat with the remaining ingredients. Serve with soy sauce, pickled ginger, and wasabi paste on the side.

inside-out rolls with beef teriyaki

ingredients

MAKES 24 PIECES

5½ oz/150 g tenderloin steak, trimmed

2 tbsp teriyaki sauce (see page 180 or use ready-made sauce)

1 tbsp vegetable oil

6 sheets of toasted nori

1 quantity freshly cooked sushi rice (see page 8)

2 scallions, shredded

3 tbsp white sesame seeds, toasted

Japanese soy sauce, pickled ginger, and wasabi paste, to serve

method

1 Beat the steak out flat using a meat mallet or rolling pin. Coat the steak in the teriyaki sauce and let marinate for 1 hour. Heat the oil in a skillet and cook the steak for 3 minutes on each side. Cut the cooked steak into strips.

2 Place a sheet of nori smooth-side down on the mat with one of the long ends toward you. With wet hands, spread a sixth of the rice evenly over the nori. Lay a sheet of plastic wrap on top and turn the whole thing over so that the plastic wrap is under the rice and the nori side faces upward.

3 Arrange a sixth of the beef teriyaki across the nori at the end nearest to you. Top with shredded scallion, and sprinkle with ½ tsp of the sesame seeds.

4 Pick up the nearest edge of the rolling mat and slowly roll the mat away from you to wrap the rice-covered nori around the filling. Lift the mat and plastic wrap out of the way as you go. Spread 2 tbsp of the sesame seeds on a plate and roll the sushi in it to coat the rice.

5 Transfer the roll to a chopping board, seam-side down. Cut it into 4 even-size pieces with a wet, very sharp knife. Repeat with the remaining ingredients. Serve with soy sauce, pickled ginger, and wasabi paste.

cucumber rolls with sesame

ingredients

MAKES 24 PIECES

2 sheets of toasted nori
1/2 quantity freshly cooked
    sushi rice (see page 8)
wasabi paste
4 tsp white sesame seeds,
    toasted
1/3 English cucumber, seeded
    and cut into sticks about
    1/4 in/5 mm square
Japanese soy sauce and
    pickled ginger, to serve

method

1 Fold a nori sheet in half lengthwise, press all along the fold, and tear it into 2 equal pieces. Place a half-sheet smooth-side down on a sushi rolling mat so that one of the long edges is directly in front of you.

2 With wet hands, spread a quarter of the rice over the nori, leaving a 1/2-inch/1-cm clear border along the furthest edge.

3 Dab a small amount of wasabi in a line across the rice at the end nearest to you. Sprinkle with 1 tsp of the sesame seeds and top with strips of cucumber, arranged in a continuous line.

4 Pick up the nearest edge of the rolling mat. Slowly roll the mat away from you to wrap the nori around the filling. Use gentle, even pressure and lift the mat out of the way as you go. Press the roll onto the uncovered border of the nori to seal it.

5 Transfer the roll to a chopping board, seam-side down. Cut it in half and then cut each half into 3 equal pieces using a wet, very sharp knife. Make 3 more rolls with the remaining ingredients. Serve with soy sauce, pickled ginger, and more wasabi paste.

pickled radish & kampyo rolls

ingredients

MAKES 24 PIECES

2 sheets of toasted nori

½ quantity freshly cooked sushi rice (see page 8)

4 strips of takuan (pickled radish), ½ inch/1 cm square and 8 inch/20 cm long

Japanese soy sauce, pickled ginger, and wasabi paste, to serve

spiced kampyo

½ oz/15 g kampyo (dried gourd)

6 fl oz/175 ml/¾ cup dashi stock (see page 194 or use instant granules)

1 tbsp superfine sugar

1 tbsp Japanese soy sauce

method

1 Gently rub the kampyo with salt under running water to soften. Rinse, then soak for 2 hours in fresh water. Place in a small pan, cover with water, and let simmer for 10 minutes. Drain, then return to the pan with the seasoning ingredients. Bring to a boil, then let simmer for 15 minutes or until the ribbons are soft. Let cool, then cut 4 x 8-inch/20-cm lengths.

2 Fold a nori sheet in half lengthwise, press all along the fold, and tear it into 2 equal pieces. Place a half-sheet smooth-side down on a sushi rolling mat so that one of the long edges is directly in front of you.

3 With wet hands, spread a quarter of the rice over the nori, leaving a ½-inch/1-cm clear border along the furthest edge. Place a strip of takuan across the rice at the end nearest to you. Top with a ribbon of kampyo.

4 Slowly roll the mat to wrap the nori around the filling, using even pressure. Press the roll onto the uncovered border to seal it. Transfer the roll to a chopping board. Cut it in half and then cut each half into 3 equal pieces using a wet, very sharp knife. Repeat with the rest of the ingredients. Serve with soy sauce, pickled ginger, and wasabi paste.

asparagus & bell pepper rolls with tahini sauce

ingredients

MAKES 24 PIECES

½ red bell pepper

4 very thin spears of asparagus

2 sheets of toasted nori

½ quantity freshly cooked sushi rice (see page 8)

tahini sauce

4 tsp tahini

1 tsp sugar

1 tsp Japanese soy sauce

1 tsp sake

method

1 Put the ingredients for the tahini sauce into a small bowl. Stir until the sugar dissolves.

2 Place the bell pepper skin-side up under a hot broiler until the skin blackens. Let cool in a sealed plastic bag or box, then remove the skin and cut the flesh into thin strips. Blanch the asparagus spears in boiling water for 1–2 minutes, then dip into ice-cold water to stop the cooking. Drain.

3 Fold a nori sheet in half lengthwise, press along the fold, and tear the sheet in half. Place a half-sheet smooth-side down on a rolling mat with one of the long sides toward you. With wet hands, spread a quarter of the rice over the nori, leaving a ½-inch/1-cm clear border along the furthest edge.

4 Spread a line of tahini sauce across the rice at the end nearest to you. Top with a sixth of the bell pepper and add 1 asparagus spear.

5 Pick up the nearest edge of the rolling mat. Slowly roll the mat away from you to wrap the nori around the filling. Press onto the clear border of nori to seal it. Transfer the roll to a chopping board and cut into 6 equal pieces using a wet, sharp knife. Repeat with the rest of the ingredients. Serve with the tahini sauce.

pinwheel rolls with mushroom & spinach

ingredients

MAKES 24 PIECES

7 oz/200 g spinach, stalks
removed

½ tsp sesame oil

4 sheets of toasted nori

1 quantity freshly cooked
sushi rice (see page 8)

wasabi paste

4 tsp pine nuts, toasted

Japanese soy sauce, pickled
ginger, and wasabi paste,
to serve

spiced mushrooms

1 oz/25 g dried shiitake
mushrooms, soaked in hot
water for 30 minutes, then
chopped finely, stems
discarded

6 fl oz/175 ml/¾ cup dashi
stock (see page 194 or
use instant granules)

1 tbsp mirin

method

1 First prepare the mushrooms. Place them in a pan with the dashi stock, bring to a boil, and let simmer for 15 minutes. Stir in the mirin and let cool in the pan. Drain well.

2 Wash the spinach and place in a pan with just the water that is clinging to the leaves. Cook for 2 minutes over medium heat to wilt. Press in a colander to squeeze out the water. Chop finely, then mix with the sesame oil.

3 Place a nori sheet smooth-side down on a rolling mat so that one of the shorter sides is toward you. With wet hands, spread a quarter of the rice over the nori, leaving a ½-inch/1-cm clear border along the furthest edge.

4 Dab a line of wasabi across the rice at the end nearest to you. Top with a quarter of the spiced mushrooms and place some of the sesame spinach alongside. Sprinkle with 1 tsp of the pine nuts.

5 Slowly roll the mat to wrap the nori tightly around the filling, creating a pinwheel effect. Press the roll onto the uncovered border of the nori to seal it. Transfer the roll to a chopping board and cut it into 6 equal pieces using a wet, very sharp knife. Repeat with the rest of the ingredients. Serve with soy sauce, pickled ginger, and wasabi.

umeboshi plum rolls

ingredients

MAKES 24 PIECES

2 sheets nori

½ quantity freshly cooked
    sushi rice (see page 8)

20 umeboshi plums, pitted
    and chopped

5 shiso leaves, finely chopped

Japanese soy sauce, pickled
    ginger, and wasabi paste,
    to serve

method

1 Fold a sheet of nori in half lengthwise, press all along the fold, and then tear into 2 pieces. Place a half-sheet smooth-side down on a rolling mat so that it lies with one of the long sides directly in front of you.

2 With wet hands, spread a quarter of the rice over the nori, leaving a ½-inch/1-cm clear border along the furthest edge.

3 Arrange a line of the chopped plums across the rice at the end nearest to you. Top with a sixth of the chopped shiso leaves.

4 Pick up the nearest edge of the rolling mat and slowly roll the mat away from you to wrap the nori around the filling. Use gentle, even pressure and lift the mat out of the way as you go. Press the roll onto the uncovered border of the nori to seal it.

5 Transfer the roll to a chopping board, seam-side down. Cut it in half and then cut each half into 3 equal pieces using a wet, very sharp knife. Make 3 more rolls with the remaining ingredients. Serve with soy sauce, pickled ginger, and wasabi paste.

rice noodle rolls with snow pea sprouts

ingredients

MAKES 24 PIECES

4 oz/115 g thin dried rice
noodles

½ red bell pepper

2 tsp rice vinegar

1 tsp sugar

pinch of salt

2 scallions, green parts finely
chopped (white parts
discarded)

4 sheets of toasted nori

wasabi paste

½ English cucumber, seeded
and cut into thin sticks

½ large carrot, cut into thin
sticks

1 oz/30 g/½ cup snow pea or
mung bean sprouts

ginger and sesame dipping
sauce (see page 226),
to serve

method

1 Cook the noodles according to the package instructions. Rinse, drain, and pat dry with paper towels. Put the bell pepper under a hot broiler until the skin blackens. Let cool in a plastic bag or box, then remove the skin and cut the flesh into thin strips.

2 Put the rice vinegar, sugar, and salt into a large bowl, and stir until the sugar dissolves. Add the cooked noodles and chopped scallions and turn to coat.

3 Place a nori sheet on a rolling mat so that one of the long sides is directly in front of you. Spread a quarter of the noodle mixture over the bottom third of the nori.

4 Dab a line of wasabi across the noodles. Top with a quarter of the roasted bell pepper strips, then add a line of cucumber sticks and a line of carrot sticks. Sprinkle the filling with a quarter of the sprouts.

5 Slowly roll the mat to wrap the nori around the filling. Press the roll onto the uncovered border of the nori to seal it. Transfer the roll to a chopping board, seam-side down. Cut it into 6 equal pieces using a wet, very sharp knife. Repeat with the remaining ingredients. Serve with the Ginger and Sesame Sauce.

asparagus & omelet rolls

ingredients

MAKES 6–8 PIECES

8 thin asparagus spears

4 eggs

1 tbsp water

1 tbsp mirin

1 tsp soy sauce

½ tbsp vegetable oil

ponzu dipping sauce, to serve
    (see page 228)

method

1 Lay the asparagus spears flat in a skillet filled with simmering water and cook for 3 minutes or until tender. Cut into $3\frac{1}{2}$-inch/ 9-cm lengths and let cool.

2 Whisk the eggs with the water, mirin, and soy sauce. Heat the oil in a nonstick skillet and pour in the egg mixture. Cook on one side until the top is just set, then lay the asparagus lengths in neat lines at one end of the skillet.

3 Shake the skillet to loosen the omelet, then tip the pan away from you so that the omelet slides up the side. Using 2 chopsticks, fold the omelet over the asparagus and then continue folding to make a roll.

4 Lay a sheet of plastic wrap over a rolling mat. Tip the omelet out onto the plastic wrap. Roll it up in the mat and plastic wrap and let cool. This helps it to set in shape.

5 Transfer the roll to a chopping board, seam-side down. Trim the ends and then cut the roll into $\frac{3}{4}$-inch/2-cm pieces with a wet, very sharp knife. Turn the pieces on end and arrange them on a serving plate. Serve with the ponzu dipping sauce.

omelet rolls with cream cheese & bell pepper

ingredients

MAKES 24 PIECES

1 quantity freshly cooked
   sushi rice (see page 8)
4 sheets of toasted nori
wasabi paste
2 red bell peppers, quartered
   and seeded, then broiled
   until the skin blackens,
   skinned, and sliced
3 oz/85 g cream cheese
20 chives, left whole

omelet wraps

6 eggs
1 tsp superfine sugar
2 tsp mirin
1 tsp Japanese soy sauce
¼ tsp salt
4 tsp vegetable oil

method

1 First make the omelet. Gently whisk the eggs with the sugar, mirin, soy sauce, and salt, taking care not to create large air bubbles. Strain into a pitcher.

2 Heat 1 tsp of the oil in a tamago pan or skillet. Pour in a quarter of the egg mixture, tilting the pan to coat the base. Cook over low-medium heat until the omelet is almost set, then flip it over and cook the other side. Turn it out onto a plate lined with paper towels and let cool. If you have used a skillet, trim the omelet to make a square shape.

3 Place a sheet of plastic wrap on a rolling mat. Lay the omelet on top. With wet hands, spread a quarter of the sushi rice over the omelet. Lay the nori on top, trimming to fit.

4 Dab a line of wasabi paste across the rice at the end nearest to you. Spread with a layer of cream cheese and top with roasted bell pepper slices and 5 chives. Carefully roll the mat to wrap the omelet around the filling, using gentle, even pressure.

6 Transfer the roll to a chopping board, seam-side down. Cut it into 6 equal pieces using a wet, very sharp knife. Transfer the roll to a serving dish, keeping it seam-side down. Repeat with the remaining ingredients.

sushi

wraps

Sushi hand rolls or wraps (*temaki zushi*) are cones of toasted nori filled with vinegared rice and whatever fillings you like. They are quick to prepare and are eaten with your hands so they make great snacks or party food.

Sushi wraps need to be eaten straight away since the nori loses its crispness quite quickly. For this reason, you may like to get your guests to make their own, especially if you are serving more than four people at once. Simply prepare all the ingredients beforehand, give each person a few sheets of nori, and show them how to roll their own. It's a good idea to have individual finger bowls and warm, damp towels at the ready so that your guests can wipe their hands.

Boat sushi (*gunkan maki*) are a great way to bring variety to your sushi feast. The rice is molded into an oval, then wrapped in nori, with the fillings placed on top. Boat sushi make good receptacles for soft fillings such as fish roe. Like wraps, they need to be eaten soon after making or the nori goes soft. In tofu pouches (*inari zushi*) the rice is stuffed into a ready-made tofu bag. They taste good just with plain vinegared rice, but you can vary the flavors by adding other ingredients such as pickled ginger, toasted sesame seeds, chopped mushroom, or shredded chicken.

wraps with fresh tuna, salmon roe & shiso leaves

ingredients

MAKES 6 PIECES

4 oz/115 g sashimi-grade
   tuna

3 sheets of toasted nori

¼ quantity freshly cooked
   sushi rice (see page 8)

wasabi paste

6 shiso leaves, finely chopped

2 tbsp salmon roe

Japanese soy sauce, pickled
   ginger, and wasabi paste,
   to serve

method

1 Trim the tuna and cut it into strips about ⅓ inch/8 mm thick, using a wet, very sharp knife and slicing across the grain. Wipe your knife on a damp cloth between each cut.

2 Fold a sheet of nori in half lengthwise, press along the fold, and then tear it into 2 pieces. Put the half you are not using straight away back into the package or cover it with plastic wrap so that it does not dry out.

3 Lay the half-sheet of nori smooth-side down on a work surface and place a heaping tbsp of rice on the left-hand side. Dab the rice with a little wasabi paste. Top with a sixth of the tuna, then add a sixth of the chopped shiso leaves.

4 Fold the bottom left-hand corner of the nori over the rice and filling, so that the folded edge forms a right angle with the bottom edge. Continue folding along that line to make a cone with a sharp point at the bottom. Place a drop of vinegared water on the underside of the join to seal it.

5 Put 1 tsp of the salmon roe in the cone to garnish. Repeat with the rest of the ingredients to make 6 cones in total. Serve with soy sauce, pickled ginger, and wasabi paste on the side.

glazed eel hand rolls

ingredients

MAKES 6 PIECES

4 fl oz/125 ml/½ cup
　　Japanese soy sauce

2 tbsp mirin

2 tbsp sake

honey, to taste

3 sheets of toasted nori

¼ quantity freshly cooked
　　sushi rice (see page 8)

2 smoked eel fillets, cut into
　　strips lengthwise

½ ripe avocado, pitted,
　　peeled, and cut into slices

Japanese soy sauce, pickled
　　ginger, and wasabi paste,
　　to serve

method

1 Put the soy sauce, mirin, and sake in a pan and let simmer for 5 minutes, or until slightly thickened. Stir in a teaspoon of honey, adding more to taste if liked. Let cool.

2 Fold a sheet of nori in half lengthwise, press along the fold, and then tear it into 2 pieces. Put the half you are not using straight away back into the package or cover it with plastic wrap so that it does not dry out.

3 Lay a half-sheet of nori, smooth-side down, on a work surface and place a heaping tbsp of rice on the left-hand side. Lay a sixth of the eel strips over the rice and drizzle with some of the prepared sauce. Add 2 slices of avocado.

4 Fold the bottom left-hand corner of the nori over the rice and filling, so that the folded edge forms a right angle with the bottom edge. Continue folding along that line to make a cone with a sharp point at the bottom. Place a drop of vinegared water on the underside of the join to seal it.

5 Repeat with the rest of the ingredients to make 6 cones in total. Serve with soy sauce, pickled ginger, and wasabi paste.

salmon, cucumber & pickled radish wraps

ingredients

MAKES 6 PIECES

4 oz/115 g sashimi-grade
   salmon
3 sheets of toasted nori
¼ quantity freshly cooked
   sushi rice (see page 8)
wasabi paste
⅓ English cucumber, seeded
   and cut into thin strips
2 oz/55 g takuan (pickled
   radish), cut into thin strips
Japanese soy sauce, pickled
   ginger, and wasabi paste,
   to serve

method

1 Trim the salmon and cut into strips about ⅓ inch/8 mm thick, using a wet, very sharp knife and slicing across the grain. Wipe your knife on a damp cloth between each cut.

2 Fold a nori sheet in half lengthwise, press along the fold, and then tear it into 2 pieces. Put the half you are not using straight away back into the package or cover it with plastic wrap so that it does not dry out.

3 Lay a half-sheet of nori smooth-side down on a work surface and place a heaping tbsp of rice on the left-hand side. Dab the rice with a little wasabi paste. Top with a sixth of the salmon strips, then add a sixth of the cucumber and takuan strips.

4 Fold the bottom left-hand corner of the nori over the rice and filling, so that the folded edge forms a right angle with the bottom edge. Continue folding along that line to make a cone with a sharp point at the bottom. Place a drop of vinegared water on the underside of the join to seal it.

5 Repeat with the rest of the ingredients to make 6 cones in total. Serve with soy sauce, pickled ginger, and wasabi paste.

white fish hand rolls with tartar sauce

ingredients

MAKES 6 PIECES

¼ x 5½ oz/150 g package tempura mix

vegetable oil, for deep frying

6 oz/175 g skinless white fish, cut into ½-inch/5-mm thick strips about 2 inch/5 cm long

3 sheets of toasted nori

¼ quantity freshly cooked sushi rice (see page 8)

3 tbsp tartar sauce, plus extra to serve

3 scallions, halved lengthwise and shredded

method

1 Blend the tempura batter with water according to the package instructions. The batter should be lumpy with plenty of air bubbles. Heat the oil in a deep-fryer to 350–375°F/180–190°C, or until a cube of bread browns in 30 seconds.

2 Dip the fish strips in the batter and add to the deep-fryer 3 at a time. Fry for 2–3 minutes, until the batter is golden brown and the fish is cooked. Drain on paper towels and let cool.

3 Fold a nori sheet in half lengthwise, press along the fold, and then tear it into 2 pieces. Lay a half-sheet smooth-side down on a work surface and place a heaping tbsp of rice on the left. Spread ½ tbsp tartar sauce over the rice and then top with 2 battered fish strips. Sprinkle with a sixth of the shredded scallion.

4 Fold the bottom left-hand corner of the nori over the rice and filling, so that the folded edge forms a right angle with the bottom edge. Continue folding along that line to make a cone with a sharp point at the bottom. Place a drop of vinegared water on the underside of the join to seal it.

5 Repeat with the rest of the ingredients to make 6 cones in total. Serve with extra tartar. Sauce for dipping.

tuna tataki hand rolls

ingredients

MAKES 6 PIECES

1 tsp freshly ground black
   pepper
1 tbsp shredded fresh
   gingerroot
1 tbsp white sesame seeds
5½ oz/150 g very fresh
   tuna fillet
salt
2 tbsp vegetable oil
3 sheets of toasted nori
¼ quantity freshly cooked
   sushi rice (see page 8)
½ English cucumber, seeded
   and cut into thin sticks
4 tbsp Japanese mayonnaise
wasabi paste

method

1 Mix together the black pepper, shredded gingerroot, and sesame seeds. Rub the mixture all over the tuna, pressing the seeds on firmly. Season the tuna lightly with salt.

2 Heat the oil in a skillet until it is very hot. Cook the tuna for 4 minutes on each side, or until just cooked through. Remove from the skillet, let cool, then cut into thin slices.

3 Fold a nori sheet in half lengthwise, press along the fold, and then tear it into 2 pieces. Lay a half-sheet smooth-side down on a work surface and place a heaping tbsp of rice on the left. Lay a sixth of the tuna strips and cucumber sticks on the rice, then spoon over ⅔ tbsp of the mayonnaise and dot a little wasabi paste on top.

4 Fold the bottom left-hand corner of the nori over the rice and filling, so that the folded edge forms a right angle with the bottom edge. Continue folding along that line to make a cone with a sharp point at the bottom. Place a drop of vinegared water on the underside of the join to seal it.

5 Repeat with the rest of the ingredients to make 6 cones in total.

salt & pepper squid wraps

ingredients

MAKES 6 PIECES

4 tbsp all-purpose flour

1 tsp Szechuan pepper or
   black pepper, crushed

1 tsp sea salt, crushed

12 squid rings, membranes
   removed, cut in half

vegetable oil, for frying

3 sheets of toasted nori

¼ quantity freshly cooked
   sushi rice (see page 8)

4 tbsp Japanese mayonnaise

method

1 Mix the flour with the crushed Szechuan or black pepper and salt. Put the seasoned flour into a plastic bag with the squid, and shake until the squid is thoroughly coated.

2 Heat about $3/4$ inch/2 cm of oil in a wok until it is very hot. Add the seasoned squid in batches and cook, stirring, for 1 minute, or until the coating is browned. Drain on paper towels to get rid of any excess oil.

3 Fold a nori sheet in half lengthwise, press along the fold, and then tear it into 2 pieces. Lay a half-sheet smooth-side down on a work surface and place a heaping tbsp of rice on the left. Lay 4 cooked squid halves on the rice, and spoon over $2/3$ tbsp of the mayonnaise.

4 Fold the bottom left-hand corner of the nori over the rice and filling, so that the folded edge forms a right angle with the bottom edge. Continue folding along that line to make a cone with a sharp point at the bottom. Place a drop of vinegared water on the underside of the join to seal it.

5 Repeat with the rest of the ingredients to make 6 cones in total.

sweet chili salmon hand rolls

ingredients

MAKES 6 PIECES

5½-oz/150-g piece of salmon
   fillet, skin on
salt and black pepper
1 tbsp vegetable oil
3 sheets of toasted nori
¼ quantity freshly cooked
   sushi rice (see page 8)
2 scallions, halved lengthwise
   and shredded
4 tbsp Japanese mayonnaise
2 tbsp sweet chili sauce, plus
   extra to serve
thin cucumber sticks, to serve

method

1 Season the salmon with the salt and pepper.

2 Heat the oil in a skillet until it is very hot, then add the salmon skin-side down. Cook over high heat for 2 minutes, until the skin is crisp. Reduce the heat to medium and cook for 2 more minutes, then turn the salmon over and cook for a further minute or until the fish is cooked through. Let cool, then flake it, keeping some pieces attached to the skin.

3 Fold a nori sheet in half lengthwise, press along the fold, and tear it into 2 pieces. Lay a half-sheet smooth-side down on a work surface and place a heaping tbsp of rice on the left. Lay a sixth of the flaked salmon and shredded scallion on the rice. Spoon ⅔ tbsp of the mayonnaise over the top and dot on 1 tsp sweet chili sauce.

4 Fold the bottom left-hand corner of the nori over the rice and filling, so that the folded edge forms a right angle with the bottom edge. Continue folding along that line to make a cone with a sharp point at the bottom. Place a drop of vinegared water on the underside of the join to seal it.

5 Repeat with the rest of the ingredients to make 6 cones in total. Serve with cucumber sticks and extra sweet chili sauce.

wraps with hamachi (japanese yellowtail)

ingredients

SERVES 4

4 oz/115 g sashimi-grade
  Japanese yellowtail (or use
  red snapper)
3 sheets of toasted nori
¼ quantity freshly cooked
  sushi rice (see page 8)
handful of baby spinach
  greens
2 tbsp chopped umeboshi
  plums
¼ English cucumber, seeded
  and cut into thin sticks
2 tbsp white sesame seeds,
  toasted
Japanese soy sauce, pickled
  ginger, and wasabi paste,
  to serve

method

1 Trim the fish. Cut it into strips ⅓ inch/8 mm thick, using a wet, very sharp knife and slicing across the grain. Wipe your knife on a damp cloth between each cut.

2 Fold a nori sheet in half lengthwise, press along the fold, and then tear it into 2 pieces. Lay a half-sheet smooth-side down on a work surface and place a heaping tbsp of rice on the left-hand side. Place a few spinach greens on top of the rice and top with a sixth of the fish mixture, a sixth of the chopped umeboshi plums, and a sixth of the cucumber sticks.

3 Fold the bottom left-hand corner of the nori over the rice and filling, so that the folded edge forms a right angle with the bottom edge. Continue folding along that line to make a cone with a sharp point at the bottom. Place a drop of vinegared water on the underside of the join to seal it.

4 Sprinkle 1 tsp toasted sesame seeds over the exposed filling. Repeat with the rest of the ingredients to make 6 cones in total. Serve with soy sauce, pickled ginger, and wasabi.

shrimp tempura & lettuce wraps

ingredients

MAKES 6 PIECES

6 large raw shrimp, shelled
   and deveined
¼ x 5½ oz/150 g package
   tempura mix
vegetable oil, for deep-frying
3 sheets of toasted nori
¼ quantity freshly cooked
   sushi rice (see page 8)
handful of iceberg lettuce
   leaves, shredded
1 red and 1 green chile,
   seeded and cut into very
   fine strips (optional)
tempura dipping sauce (see
   page 204), to serve

method

1 Cut a few slits on the underside of the shrimp to keep them straight as they cook.

2 Blend the tempura batter with water according to the package instructions. The batter should be lumpy with plenty of air bubbles. Heat the vegetable oil in a deep-fryer to 350–375°F/180–190°C, or until a cube of bread browns in 30 seconds.

3 Dip the prepared shrimp in the batter mix, then drop them into the oil 3 at a time. Cook for 2–3 minutes, until golden. Remove from the oil and drain on kitchen towels. Let cool.

4 Halve the nori sheets (see page 78). Lay a half-sheet of nori smooth-side down on a work surface and place a heaping tbsp of rice on the left-hand side. Top with shredded lettuce and 1 tempura shrimp, then add a strip of red and a strip of green chile, if using.

5 Fold the bottom left-hand corner of the nori over the rice and filling, so that the folded edge forms a right angle with the bottom edge. Continue folding along that line to make a cone with a sharp point at the bottom. Place a drop of vinegared water on the underside of the join to seal it. Repeat with the rest of the ingredients to make 6 cones in total. Serve with the Tempura Dipping Sauce.

duck & hoisin hand rolls

ingredients

MAKES 6 PIECES

¼ prepared barbecued or
  Peking duck
4 tbsp hoisin or plum sauce
3 sheets of toasted nori
¼ quantity freshly cooked
  sushi rice (see page 8)
3 scallions, halved lengthwise
  and shredded, plus extra,
  to garnish

method

1 Pull the flesh and skin off the duck and slice into strips. If you have lots of skin, just keep the crispiest bits. Discard any excess fat.

2 Put half the hoisin or plum sauce into a large bowl, add the duck strips, and toss to coat.

3 Fold a nori sheet in half lengthwise, press along the fold, and then tear it into 2 pieces. Lay a half-sheet smooth-side down on a work surface and place a heaping tbsp of rice on the left-hand side. Lay a sixth of the duck and duck skin on the rice, scatter with some of the shredded scallion, then drizzle over 1 tsp of the remaining hoisin or plum sauce.

4 Fold the bottom left-hand corner of the nori over the rice and filling, so that the folded edge forms a right angle with the bottom edge. Continue folding along that line to make a cone with a sharp point at the bottom. Place a drop of vinegared water on the underside of the join to seal it.

5 Repeat with the rest of the ingredients to make 6 cones in total, transfer to a serving plate, and garnish with the remaining shredded scallions.

roast beef wraps with wasabi mayonnaise

ingredients

MAKES 6 PIECES

2 oz/55 g fresh daikon (long white radish), peeled
3 sheets of toasted nori
¼ quantity freshly cooked sushi rice (see page 8)
2 oz/55 g mizuna greens
6 thin slices rare roast beef

wasabi mayonnaise

2 tbsp mayonnaise
1 tsp wasabi paste, or to taste

method

1 Shred the daikon using the finest setting on a mandolin. Alternatively, cut it into long thin slices and then cut each slice along its length as finely as possible. Rinse, drain, and then place in the refrigerator until needed.

2 Make the wasabi mayonnaise by combining the mayonnaise and wasabi paste in a bowl.

3 Fold a nori sheet in half lengthwise, press along the fold, and then tear it into 2 pieces.

4 Lay a half-sheet of nori smooth-side down on a work surface and place a heaping tbsp of rice on the left-hand side. Spread 1 tsp wasabi mayonnaise over the rice, then add a few mizuna greens and a sixth of the chilled shredded daikon. Roll up 1 slice of beef into a cone shape and place it on top.

5 Fold the bottom left-hand corner of the nori over the rice and filling, so that the folded edge forms a right angle with the bottom edge. Continue folding along that line to make a cone with a sharp point at the bottom. Place a drop of vinegared water on the underside of the join to seal it. Repeat with the rest of the ingredients to make 6 cones in total.

avocado, watercress & pickle wraps

ingredients

MAKES 6 PIECES

3 sheets of toasted nori

¼ quantity freshly cooked
    sushi rice (see page 8)

wasabi paste

6 sprigs of watercress

¼ English cucumber, seeded
    and cut into sticks

1 ripe green-skinned
    avocado, pitted, peeled,
    and cut into 12 slices

2 oz/55 g Japanese pickle
    such as sakurazuke or
    shibazuke

18 long chives, trimmed

Japanese soy sauce, pickled
    ginger, and wasabi paste,
    to serve

method

1 Fold the nori in half lengthwise, press along the fold, and then tear the sheet into 2 pieces. Put the half you are not using straight away back into the package or cover it with plastic wrap so that it does not dry out.

2 Lay a half-sheet of nori, smooth-side down, on a work surface and place a heaping tbsp of rice on the left-hand side. Dab a little wasabi over the rice. Arrange 1 sprig of watercress, a sixth of the cucumber sticks, 2 avocado slices, and a sixth of the pickle on top. Garnish with 3 long chives.

3 Fold the bottom left-hand corner of the nori over the rice and filling, so that the folded edge forms a right angle with the bottom edge. Continue folding along that line to make a cone with a sharp point at the bottom. Place a drop of vinegared water on the underside of the join to seal it.

4 Repeat with the rest of the ingredients to make 6 cones in total. Serve with soy sauce, pickled ginger, and wasabi paste.

omelet wraps with pickled radish & shiso leaves

ingredients

MAKES 6 PIECES

¼ quantity freshly cooked
  sushi rice (see page 8)
wasabi paste
2 oz/55 g takuan (pickled
  radish), cut into thin strips
6 shiso leaves

omelet wrappings

4 eggs
1 tsp superfine sugar
2 tsp mirin
1 tsp Japanese soy sauce
¼ tsp salt
3 tsp vegetable oil

method

1 First make the omelet. Gently whisk the eggs with the sugar, mirin, soy sauce, and salt, taking care not to create large air bubbles. Strain into a pitcher.

2 Pour 1 tsp of the oil into a tamago pan or skillet, then heat over low-medium heat. Pour in ⅓ of the omelet mixture, tilting the pan to coat the base. When the omelet is almost set, flip it over and cook the other side. Turn it out onto a plate lined with paper towels and let cool. If using a round skillet, trim to make a square shape. Cut the omelet in half, to make 2 wrappings.

3 Place 1 piece of omelet on your chopping board. Spoon a heaping tbsp of sushi rice onto the left-hand side. Dab a little wasabi over the rice. Place a sixth of the takuan strips and 1 shiso leaf over the rice.

4 Fold the bottom left-hand corner of the omelet over the rice and filling, so that the folded edge forms a right angle with the bottom edge. Continue folding along that line to make a cone that ends in a point.

5 Serve straight away while you use the rest of the ingredients to make the remaining rolls.

classic sushi boat with salmon roe

ingredients

MAKES 8 PIECES

⅓ quantity freshly cooked
  sushi rice (see page 8)
2 sheets of toasted nori, each
  cut into 4 strips lengthwise
wasabi paste
8 tbsp salmon, trout, or flying
  fish roe
soy sauce and pickled ginger,
  to serve

method

1 Divide the rice into 8 equal batches. Wet your hands to stop the rice sticking, then shape each batch of rice into an oval. Carefully wrap a strip of nori round each oval of rice and trim off any excess. Place a drop of vinegared water on the underside of the join to seal it.

2 Dab a little wasabi on top of each sushi boat and top with 1 tbsp of the salmon roe. Repeat with the rest of the ingredients. Serve with soy sauce, pickled ginger, and more wasabi paste on the side.

smoked trout sushi boat

ingredients

MAKES 8 PIECES

⅓ quantity freshly cooked
    sushi rice (see page 8)
2 sheets of toasted nori, each
    cut into 4 strips lengthwise
2 tbsp Japanese mayonnaise
1 tsp grated lemon zest
2 tsp lemon juice
2 scallions, finely chopped
1 smoked trout fillet, flaked
2 oz/55 g smoked salmon,
    cut into strips
ponzu dipping sauce (see
    page 228), to serve

method

1 Divide the rice into 8 equal batches. Wet your hands to stop the rice sticking, then shape each batch of rice into a neat oval. Carefully wrap a strip of nori round each oval of rice, trimming off any excess. Place a drop of vinegared water on the underside of the join to seal it.

2 Mix the mayonnaise with the lemon zest and juice. Spread 1 tsp of the mixture on top of each sushi boat. Sprinkle with some chopped scallion, then top with a sixth of the flaked smoked trout and a sixth of the smoked salmon. Serve with the ponzu dipping sauce.

lemon pepper crab sushi boat

ingredients

MAKES 8 PIECES

1 small cooked prepared crab

1 tsp grated lemon zest

2 tbsp Japanese mayonnaise

salt and black pepper

⅓ quantity freshly cooked
   sushi rice (see page 8)

2 sheets of toasted nori, each
   cut into 4 strips lengthwise

juice of 1 lemon

2 lemons, cut into wedges,
   to garnish

method

1 Lift the crabmeat out of the shell and mix with the grated lemon zest and mayonnaise. Season with salt and plenty of black pepper.

2 Divide the rice into 8 equal batches. Wet your hands to stop the rice sticking, then shape each batch of the rice into an oval. Carefully wrap a strip of nori round each oval of rice, trimming off any excess. Place a drop of vinegared water on the underside of the join to seal it.

3 Top the sushi boat with a sixth of the crab mixture, then squeeze over a few drops of lemon juice. Repeat with the remaining ingredients, and serve with lemon wedges on the side.

green bean sushi boats

ingredients

MAKES 8 PIECES

20 green beans, trimmed and
   finely sliced
1 tbsp sesame oil
1 tbsp white sesame seeds,
   toasted
salt and black pepper
1 tsp grated lemon zest
⅓ quantity freshly cooked
   sushi rice (see page 8)
2 sheets of toasted nori, each
   cut into 4 strips lengthwise
wasabi paste
soy sauce and pickled ginger,
   to serve

method

1 Put the green beans in a pan with a little water and bring to a boil. Cook for 2 minutes, then drain and toss with the sesame oil and toasted sesame seeds. Season with salt and pepper to taste, and mix in the lemon zest.

2 Divide the rice into 8 equal batches. Wet your hands to stop the rice sticking, then shape each batch into an oval using your hands. Carefully wrap a strip of nori round each oval of rice, trimming off any excess. Place a drop of vinegared water on the underside of the join to seal it.

3 Dab a little wasabi on top of each sushi boat and top with the green beans. Repeat with the rest of the ingredients. Serve with soy sauce, pickled ginger, and more wasabi paste.

sweet tofu pouches

ingredients

MAKES 8 PIECES

4 abura-age (deep-fried tofu)
6 fl oz/175 ml/¾ cup dashi
    stock (see page 194 or
    use instant granules)
3 tbsp soy sauce
2 tbsp superfine sugar
1 tbsp sake
1 tbsp sesame seeds, toasted
¼ quantity freshly cooked
    sushi rice (see page 8)

method

1 Put the tofu into a bowl and pour boiling water over it to remove any excess oil. Drain and let cool. Cut each piece in half and gently open out each half into a bag.

2 Place the dashi stock, soy sauce, sugar, and sake in a pan, stir, and bring to a boil. Add the tofu bags, and let simmer for 10–15 minutes until almost all the liquid has been absorbed. Remove from the heat, drain, and let cool. Press any remaining liquid out of the bags with a clean dish towel (the bags should be moist but not wet).

3 Gently mix the toasted sesame seeds with the sushi rice. Fill the bags with the rice mixture and fold over the tops to enclose them. Serve at room temperature.

shredded chile chicken pouches

ingredients

MAKES 8 PIECES

4 sheets of abura-age (deep-fried tofu)

6 fl oz/175 ml/¾ cup dashi stock (see page 194 or use instant granules)

3 tbsp Japanese soy sauce

2 tbsp superfine sugar

1 tbsp sake

1 skinless, boneless chicken breast, about 5½ oz/150 g

1 tbsp vegetable oil

1 tsp red chile flakes

2 tbsp pine nuts, toasted

1 tbsp chopped flat-leaf parsley

¼ quantity freshly cooked sushi rice (see page 8)

method

1 Put the tofu in a bowl and pour boiling water over it to remove any excess oil. Drain and let cool. Cut each piece in half and gently open out each half into a bag.

2 Place the dashi stock, soy sauce, sugar, and sake in a pan, stir, and bring to a boil. Add the tofu bags and let simmer for 10–15 minutes, until almost all the liquid has been absorbed. Remove from the heat, drain, and let cool. Press any remaining liquid out of the bags with a clean dish towel (the bags should be moist but not wet).

3 While the bags are simmering, cut the chicken into thin strips. Heat the oil in a wok or large skillet, then add the chile flakes. Heat for a few seconds, then add the chicken strips. Cook for 3–4 minutes, until the chicken is cooked through. Drain on kitchen towels and then chop very finely. Let cool.

4 Gently stir the chile chicken, toasted pine nuts, and parsley into the sushi rice. Fill the seasoned tofu bags with the rice mixture and fold over the tops to enclose them. Serve them at room temperature.

omelet pouches with mushroom

ingredients

MAKES 6 PIECES

½ oz/15 g butter

8 oz/225 g fresh mushrooms such as oyster or shiitake, sliced

¼ quantity freshly cooked sushi rice (see page 8)

1 tbsp finely chopped flat-leaf parsley

pinch of cayenne pepper

6 long chives

Japanese soy sauce, pickled ginger, and wasabi paste, to serve

omelet wrappings

4 eggs

1 tsp superfine sugar

2 tsp mirin

1 tsp Japanese soy sauce

¼ tsp salt

4 tsp vegetable oil

method

1 Melt the butter in a small pan. When it is sizzling, add the sliced mushrooms and cook over high heat for 3–4 minutes until browned and reduced by half in volume.

2 Remove the mushrooms with a slotted spoon and chop finely. Mix with the rice, chopped parsley, and cayenne pepper.

3 Now make the omelet wrappings. Gently whisk the eggs with the sugar, mirin, soy sauce, and salt, taking care not to produce any large air bubbles. Strain into a pitcher.

4 Pour ⅔ tsp of the oil into a 6-inch/15-cm skillet, then heat over low-medium heat. Pour in a sixth of the omelet mixture, tilting the pan to coat the base. When the omelet is almost set, flip it over and cook the other side. Turn out onto a plate lined with paper towels and let cool.

5 Transfer 1 omelet to your work surface and place a sixth of the mushroom and rice mixture in the center. Gather up the 4 corners of the omelet and tie them together using a long chive. Serve with soy sauce, pickled ginger, and wasabi paste.

sashimi, pressed sushi & finger sushi

A large part of the appeal of sushi is its precise, almost geometric appearance. It isn't difficult to make raw fish slices (*sashimi*) look neat, but it takes a little practice. For pressed sushi (*oshi sushi*) it is worth getting a sushi press. Choose between a traditional wooden version, which needs to be soaked for 15 minutes before use, or a plastic one, which can simply be dampened with a clean, wet cloth. Sushi presses come in different sizes—the one used in these recipes makes 5 pieces at a time.

If you don't have a press, you can use a loose-bottomed 7-inch/8-cm cake pan, which will make 15 sushi in one go. You'll need to use $\frac{3}{4}$ quantity of the sushi rice and increase the other ingredients in each recipe by half to ensure that you have enough to cover the pan. Line the pan with a large sheet of plastic wrap before adding the filling and topping. Cover it with the overhanging wrap, place another pan on top, and weigh it down with a couple of cans. Leave for 15 minutes, then remove the weights and pan, and pull up the sides of the pan or pull on the plastic wrap to release the sushi.

Finger sushi (*nigiri sushi*) is most easily made with a finger sushi mold, or you can shape rice blocks by hand, like the professionals do. Have a bowl of water to which you've added a little rice vinegar nearby so that you can wet your hands before handling the rice.

mixed sashimi

ingredients

SERVES 2

1 fresh mackerel, cleaned
and filleted

3½ fl oz/100 ml/generous
⅓ cup rice vinegar

3 raw scallops, in their shells

5½ oz/150 g sashimi-grade
tuna, trimmed

5½ oz/150 g sashimi-grade
salmon, trimmed

2 oz/55 g daikon (long white
radish), shredded

whole trimmed chives and
shiso leaves, to garnish

wasabi paste, Japanese
soy sauce, and pickled
ginger, to serve

method

1 Place the mackerel fillets in a shallow, non-metallic dish, pour over the rice vinegar, and cover with plastic wrap. Let marinate in the refrigerator for 1 hour.

2 Remove the mackerel from the marinade, pat dry with paper towels, and take off the skin. Holding a wet, very sharp knife at a 45° angle to the chopping board, cut the fish into ⅓-inch/8-mm thick, diagonal slices.

3 To prepare the scallops, insert a short, strong knife between the shells and twist to prise apart. Separate the scallops from their shells. Remove and discard any corals and black matter, the white frills, and membranes. Slice the scallops in half horizontally.

4 Put the halved scallops into a heatproof dish and cover with boiling water. Remove with a slotted spoon straight away. Pat the scallops dry with paper towels.

5 Slice the tuna and salmon into ⅓-inch/8-mm thick rectangles, using a wet, very sharp knife and cutting across the grain. Wipe your knife on a damp cloth between each cut.

6 Place the shredded daikon on a serving platter, place the scallops on top, and arrange the sliced fish around it. Garnish with fresh chives. Add a mound of wasabi paste and serve with soy sauce and pickled ginger.

sea bass with chili oil

ingredients

SERVES 4

2 oz/55 g daikon (long white
    radish)

1 small fresh sea bass, scaled
    and filleted

small handful of baby salad
    greens

2 tsp chili oil

Japanese soy sauce, pickled
    ginger, and wasabi paste,
    to serve

method

1 Shred the daikon using the finest setting on a mandolin. Alternatively, cut it into long thin slices and then cut each slice along its length as finely as possible. Rinse, drain, and then place in the refrigerator until needed.

2 Trim the sea-bass fillets into neat rectangles, and place skinned-side up on a chopping board. Cut each fillet into oblongs $1/3$ inch/8 mm thick, using a wet, very sharp knife and slicing across the grain. Wipe your knife on a damp cloth between each cut.

3 Place a few baby salad greens on 4 serving plates and top with a heap of shredded daikon. Arrange the sea bass slices so that they overlap slightly in a fan-shape, and drizzle with the chili oil. Serve with soy sauce, pickled ginger, and wasabi.

seared swordfish salad

ingredients

SERVES 4

3 oz/85 g daikon (long white) radish

2 oz/55 g carrot

½ English cucumber

9 oz/250 g fresh swordfish steak, skinned

2 tsp peanut oil

2 tsp white sesame seeds, toasted

sesame dressing

1 tbsp Japanese soy sauce

2 tbsp sesame oil

½ tsp wasabi paste

1 tsp rice vinegar

method

1 Place all the ingredients for the sesame dressing in a small bowl and stir to combine. Refrigerate until needed.

2 Shred the daikon and carrot using the finest setting on a mandolin. Alternatively, cut it into long thin slices and then cut each slice along its length as finely as possible. Rinse, drain, and then place in the refrigerator until needed. Shred the cucumber, discarding the seeded parts. Add to the daikon and carrot.

3 Trim the swordfish steak. Heat the oil in a skillet until very hot, then sear the swordfish for 30–60 seconds on both sides and the edges. Let cool.

4 Cut the seared swordfish into ⅓-inch/8-mm thick pieces, using a wet, very sharp knife and slicing across the grain. Wipe your knife on a damp cloth between each cut.

5 Arrange the fish slices on 4 serving plates and place a mound of the shredded salad vegetables alongside. Drizzle the salad vegetables with the sesame dressing and sprinkle with the toasted sesame seeds.

marinated tuna sashimi

ingredients

SERVES 4

14 oz/400 g sashimi-grade
tuna

3 tsp wasabi paste

4 tbsp Japanese soy sauce

1 tbsp chopped chives, to
garnish

method

1 Trim the tuna. Slice into $\frac{1}{2}$-inch/1-cm thick rectangles, using a wet, very sharp knife and cutting across the grain. Wipe your knife on a damp cloth between each cut.

2 Place the wasabi and soy sauce in a bowl that is large enough to take the tuna and stir well to combine. Add the sliced tuna, and turn to coat. Let marinate for 5 minutes.

3 Arrange the marinated tuna slices on 4 serving plates and garnish with the chives.

seared salmon sashimi with sesame & black pepper

ingredients

SERVES 4

2 oz/55 g daikon (long white radish)

3 oz/85 g white sesame seeds

black pepper

14 oz/400 g sashimi-grade salmon

2 tsp peanut oil

4 shiso leaves

ponzu dipping sauce (see page 228), to serve

method

1 Shred the daikon using the finest setting on a mandolin. Alternatively, cut it into long thin slices and then cut each slice along its length as finely as possible. Rinse, drain, and then place in the refrigerator until needed.

2 Crush the sesame seeds in a mortar and pestle and spread over a large plate. Grind over plenty of black pepper and stir to mix.

3 Trim the salmon fillet into a neat rectangle. Heat the oil in a skillet until very hot. Sear the salmon for 1 minute on both sides and the edges, then remove from the pan.

4 Lay the salmon on the sesame and pepper mixture, and turn to coat evenly. Use a wet, very sharp knife to cut the seared salmon into 1/3-inch/8-mm thick oblongs, slicing across the grain. Wipe your knife on a damp cloth between each cut.

5 Arrange the slices on 4 serving plates. Place a shiso leaf on each plate and top with a quarter of the shredded daikon. Serve with the Ponzu Dipping Sauce.

tuna & cucumber pressed sushi

ingredients

MAKES 10 PIECES

6 oz/175 g sashimi-grade
tuna, trimmed

1 English cucumber

½ quantity freshly cooked
sushi rice (see page 8)

wasabi paste

Japanese soy sauce, pickled
ginger, and wasabi paste,
to serve

method

1 Cut the tuna into ¼-inch/5-mm thick pieces with a wet, very sharp knife, slicing across the grain. Place in the refrigerator until needed.

2 Cut the cucumber in half lengthways. Reserve half for use in another recipe and use a teaspoon to scoop out the seeds from the remaining half. Slice the deseeded half-cucumber into ribbons using a mandolin or vegetable peeler, then trim the ribbons to the length of the sushi press.

3 Wet the sushi press. Add a layer of tuna slices, covering the bottom entirely. Dab a little wasabi paste over the tuna, then cover with a quarter of the sushi rice. Press down with the lid.

4 Cover the rice with a layer of cucumber and top with another quarter of the sushi rice. Press down again.

5 Lift off the sides of the sushi press, holding down the lid with your thumbs as you do so. Turn the sushi out onto a chopping board so that the fish layer is on top, and cut into 5 equal slices using a wet, very sharp knife. Repeat, to make 10 pieces in total. Serve with soy sauce, pickled ginger, and wasabi paste.

smoked salmon sushi balls

ingredients

MAKES 10 PIECES

1 or 2 slices of smoked
    salmon
juice of ¼ lemon
¼ quantity freshly cooked
    sushi rice (see page 8)
wasabi paste
lemon zest, to garnish
Japanese soy sauce, pickled
    ginger, and wasabi paste,
    to serve

method

1 Cut the salmon into 10 small pieces about 1 inch/2.5 cm square, then squeeze the lemon juice over the top.

2 Cut a square of plastic wrap measuring 4 inch x 4 inch/10 cm x 10 cm. Place 1 piece of smoked salmon in the center of the wrap.

3 Take 1½ tsp sushi rice and gently roll it into a ball. Lay it on top of the salmon.

4 Wrap the plastic wrap around the rice and salmon, twisting the 4 corners together to form a tight package so that the rice inside makes a smooth ball. Repeat to make 10 balls in total.

5 Unwrap the balls just before serving. Put a dab of wasabi and a tiny strip of lemon zest on top of each ball to garnish. Serve with soy sauce, pickled ginger, and wasabi paste.

marinated mackerel sushi

ingredients

MAKES 10 PIECES

2 mackerel fillets, about
    5 oz/140 g each
3 tbsp sea salt
8 fl oz/250 ml/1 cup rice
    vinegar
wasabi paste
½ quantity freshly cooked
    sushi rice (see page 8)
Japanese soy sauce and
    pickled ginger, to serve

method

1 Lay the mackerel fillets in a dish. Sprinkle with the salt, then gently rub it into the flesh and skin. Refrigerate for 2 hours.

2 Rinse the salted mackerel under running water and pat dry with kitchen towels. Place the fillets side by side in a shallow dish and pour over the rice vinegar. Marinate for 1 hour in the refrigerator.

3 Pat the fillets dry. Lift the papery outer skin at one end and peel it off, leaving the silvery underskin intact. Use a pair of tweezers to remove any small bones. Trim the top of the flesh with a sharp knife so that the fillets have an even thickness.

4 Wet a sushi press to stop the rice from sticking. Place the fillets in the mold, skin-side down, trimming them so that they cover the bottom with no gaps. Dab a little wasabi over the top, then pack in half of the rice. Press down with the lid.

5 Lift off the sides of the sushi press, holding down the lid with your thumbs as you do so. Turn the sushi out onto a chopping board so that the fish is on top, and cut into 5 equal slices. Repeat, to make 10 pieces in total. Serve with soy sauce, pickled ginger, and extra wasabi paste on the side.

red snapper finger sushi

ingredients

MAKES 10 PIECES

6 oz/175 g red snapper fillets
½ quantity freshly cooked
    sushi rice (see page 8)
wasabi paste
Japanese soy sauce and
    pickled ginger, to serve

method

1 Place the red snapper on a chopping board. Holding a very sharp knife at a 45° angle to the chopping board, cut the fish into diagonal, ¼-inch/5-mm thick slices. Your slices should be about 3 inch/7.5 cm long and 1¼ inch/3 cm wide so that they can be draped over the smaller rice blocks. Refrigerate until needed.

2 Wet a finger sushi mold to stop the rice from sticking. Fill each section with sushi rice, working the rice into the corners without pressing too hard. Press down with the lid, then remove it, and turn the neat blocks out onto a chopping board. Repeat so that you have 10 blocks.

3 Alternatively, shape the rice by hand. Take a golfball-sized amount of rice in the palm of one hand, then gently press it into an oblong, using your palm and the fingers of your other hand. The block should be 2 inch/5 cm long and ¾ inch/2 cm wide. Repeat to make 10 blocks, and place on a chopping board.

4 Dab a little wasabi paste onto each block of rice. Lay a slice of fish on top, pressing it onto the short ends of the rice block to keep it in place. Serve with soy sauce, pickled ginger, and extra wasabi.

sushi with smoked salmon & cucumber

ingredients

MAKES 10 PIECES

7 oz/200 g smoked salmon,
cut into strips

½ English cucumber, peeled
and very thinly sliced

2 tbsp Japanese mayonnaise

½ quantity freshly cooked
sushi rice (see page 8)

2 lemons, cut into wedges,
and mint sprigs, to garnish

Japanese soy sauce, pickled
ginger, and wasabi paste,
to serve

method

1 Wet a sushi press to stop the rice from sticking to it. Arrange half the smoked salmon and cucumber in diagonal strips over the bottom. Spread 1 tbsp of the mayonnaise over the top, then add half the sushi rice. Press down firmly with the lid.

2 Lift off the sides of the sushi press, holding down the lid with your thumbs as you do so. Turn the sushi out onto a chopping board so that the layer of salmon and cucumber is on top. Cut into 5 equal slices using a wet, very sharp knife. Wipe your knife on a damp cloth between cuts to keep your slices neat. Repeat, to make 10 pieces in total.

3 Arrange on a serving plate, garnished with lemon wedges and mint sprigs. Serve with soy sauce, pickled ginger, and wasabi paste.

glazed eel sushi

ingredients

MAKES 10 PIECES

12 oz/350 g ready-prepared
glazed eel
½ quantity freshly cooked
sushi rice (see page 8)
Japanese soy sauce, pickled
ginger, and wasabi paste,
to serve

method

1 Wet a sushi press to stop the rice from sticking to the sides.

2 Cut the eel into strips lengthwise. Lay the strips evenly in the sushi press, covering the bottom completely. Add half of the sushi rice, then press down with the lid.

3 Lift off the sides of the sushi press, holding down the lid with your thumbs as you do so. Turn the sushi out onto a chopping board so that the fish layer is on top, and slice into 5 equal pieces using a wet, very sharp knife. Wipe your knife on a damp cloth between each cut to keep the slices neat. Repeat, to make 10 pieces in total. Serve with soy sauce, pickled ginger, and wasabi paste on the side.

teriyaki tuna sushi with green bean strips

ingredients

MAKES 10 PIECES

7 oz/200 g tuna fillet, thinly sliced

2 tbsp teriyaki sauce (see page 180 or use ready-made sauce)

1 tbsp vegetable oil

10 green beans, trimmed and cut in half

2 tbsp Japanese mayonnaise

½ quantity freshly cooked sushi rice (see page 8)

1 tsp white sesame seeds, toasted

Japanese soy sauce, pickled ginger, and wasabi paste, to serve

method

1 Coat the tuna slices in the teriyaki sauce. Heat the oil in a skillet, then cook the coated tuna slices for 1 minute on each side, until cooked through. Cut into thick strips.

2 Blanch the green beans in boiling water for 1 minute, then plunge into ice-cold water to stop the cooking. Drain.

3 Wet a sushi press to stop the rice from sticking. Arrange the cooked tuna in 2 wide strips over the bottom, trimming it to fit, and place a line of green beans down the center. Spread 1 tbsp of the mayonnaise over the tuna and beans, then pack in half the sushi rice. Press down with the lid.

4 Lift off the sides of the sushi press, holding down the lid with your thumbs as you do so. Turn the sushi out onto a chopping board so that the layer of tuna and beans is on top, and slice into 5 equal pieces using a wet, very sharp knife. Wipe your knife on a damp cloth between each cut to keep the pieces neat. Repeat, so that you have 10 pieces in total.

5 Sprinkle the sushi with the toasted sesame seeds, and serve with soy sauce, pickled ginger, and wasabi paste.

halibut & roasted yellow bell pepper sushi

ingredients

MAKES 10 PIECES

2 yellow or orange bell peppers, quartered and seeded

½ sheet of toasted nori

6 oz/175 g sashimi-grade halibut

½ quantity freshly cooked sushi rice (see page 8)

1 red chile, cut into thin rounds, to garnish

method

1 Place the quartered bell peppers skin-side up under a hot broiler until the skin blackens. Let cool in a sealed plastic bag or box, peel off the skin, and cut the flesh into thick strips. Cut the half-sheet of nori into 10 strips.

2 Place the halibut on a chopping board. Holding a very sharp knife at a 45° angle to the chopping board, cut into diagonal, ¼-inch/5-mm thick slices, 3 inch/7.5 cm long and 1¼ inch/3 cm wide (they need to be slightly larger than the rice blocks). Refrigerate.

3 Wet a finger sushi press. Fill each section with sushi rice, working the rice into the corners. Press down with the lid, then remove it, and turn the blocks out onto a chopping board. Repeat so that you have 10 blocks. Alternatively, shape the rice by hand (see page 122).

4 Place a strip of bell pepper on each rice block. Drape a slice of halibut lengthwise over the top. Use your thumb and index finger to press it onto either end of the rice block.

5 Wrap a nori strip neatly around each sushi, tucking the ends under the rice block. Garnish with the chile rounds, and serve.

salmon & avocado sushi with lemon mayonnaise

ingredients

MAKES 10 PIECES

2 tbsp Japanese mayonnaise

2 tsp lemon zest

5½ oz/150 g smoked salmon, cut into strips

1 large ripe avocado, pitted, peeled, and cut into thin slices

½ quantity freshly cooked sushi rice (see page 8)

pickled ginger and wasabi paste, to serve

method

1 Wet a sushi press to stop the rice from sticking. Mix together the mayonnaise and lemon zest.

2 Arrange the smoked salmon and avocado in wide diagonal strips over the bottom of the sushi press. Smear 1 tbsp of the lemon mayonnaise over the top, then pack in half of the rice. Press down with the lid.

3 Lift off the sides of the sushi press, holding down the lid with your thumbs as you do so. Turn the sushi out onto a chopping board so that the fish layer is on top. Slice into 5 equal pieces using a wet, very sharp knife. Wet your knife between cuts to keep your sushi bars neat. Repeat, to make 10 pieces in total.

4 Serve the sushi with pickled ginger and wasabi paste on the side.

cooked shrimp sushi

ingredients

MAKES 10 PIECES

10 large raw shrimp, heads
    removed
1 tbsp sake
½ tsp salt
1 tbsp rice vinegar
½ quantity freshly cooked
    sushi rice (see page 8)
wasabi paste
Japanese soy sauce and
    pickled ginger, to serve

method

1 Insert a thin wooden skewer along the underside of each shrimp to prevent it from curling as it cooks. Place 1 inch/2.5 cm water in a large pan, add the sake and salt, and bring to a boil. Add the skewered shrimps and let simmer for 2 minutes until they turn pink. Drain and let cool.

2 Peel each shrimp, then cut along the back of the body and scrape out the intestinal thread. Deepen the incision and carefully open the shrimp into a flat butterfly-shape. Sprinkle with the rice vinegar and place in the refrigerator.

3 Wet a finger sushi mold. Fill each section with sushi rice, working the rice into the corners. Press down with the lid, then remove it, and turn the blocks out onto a chopping board. Repeat so that you have 10 blocks.

4 Alternatively, shape the rice by hand. Take a golfball-sized amount of rice in the palm of one hand, then gently press it into an oblong, using your palm and the fingers of your other hand. The block should be 2 inch/5 cm long and ¾ inch/2 cm wide. Repeat to make 10 blocks, and place on a chopping board.

5 Dab a little wasabi paste in the center of each rice block, then lay a butterflied shrimp on top. Serve with soy sauce, pickled ginger, and extra wasabi paste.

seared scallop sushi

ingredients

MAKES 10 PIECES

½ quantity freshly cooked
    sushi rice (see page 8)
1–2 tsp vegetable oil
3 or 4 fresh scallops
wasabi paste
Japanese soy sauce and
    pickled ginger, to serve

method

1 Wet a finger sushi mold to stop the rice from sticking to it. Fill each section with sushi rice, working the rice into the corners without pressing too hard. Press down with the lid, then remove it, and turn the neat blocks out onto a chopping board. Repeat so that you have 10 blocks in total.

2 Alternatively, shape the rice by hand. Take a golfball-sized amount of rice in the palm of one hand, then gently press it into an oblong, using your palm and the fingers of your other hand. The block should be 2 inch/5 cm long and ¾ inch/2 cm wide. Repeat to make 10 blocks, and place on a chopping board.

3 Add the oil to a skillet, tilt the pan so that the oil covers the bottom, and then wipe with a kitchen towel to remove any excess. Heat over high heat. Add the scallops and sear for 30 seconds on each side, until golden. Cut the cooked scallops into thin slices, and let cool.

4 Dab a small amount of wasabi onto the center of each rice block, then arrange the scallop slices on top. Serve with soy sauce, pickled ginger, and extra wasabi paste.

sushi balls with shrimp & flying fish roe

ingredients

MAKES 10 PIECES

10 cooked shrimp

¼ quantity freshly cooked sushi rice (see page 8)

¾ oz/20 g flying fish or other red roe

Japanese soy sauce, pickled ginger, and wasabi paste, to serve

method

1 Cut a square of plastic wrap measuring 4 inch x 4 inch/10 cm x 10 cm. Place 1 cooked shrimp in the center.

2 Take 1½ tsp sushi rice and gently roll into a ball. Lay it on top of the shrimp.

3 Wrap the plastic wrap around the rice and shrimp, twisting the 4 corners to form a tight package so that the rice inside makes a smooth ball. Repeat to make 10 balls in total.

4 Unwrap the balls just before serving, and fill the curve of each shrimp with a little flying fish or other red roe. Serve with soy sauce, pickled ginger, and wasabi paste on the side.

pressed california sushi

ingredients

MAKES 10 PIECES

1 cooked, prepared crab
½ avocado, pitted, peeled,
    and cut into thin slices
⅓ English cucumber, peeled
    and very thinly sliced
2 tbsp Japanese mayonnaise
½ quantity freshly cooked
    sushi rice (see page 8)
1 tsp sesame seeds, toasted
pickled ginger, lemon slices,
    and sprigs of dill, to
    garnish
wasabi paste, to serve

method

1 Remove the crabmeat from the shell.

2 Wet a sushi press. Arrange the crabmeat, avocado slices, and cucumber slices in wide strips over the bottom of the press. Spread 1 tbsp of the mayonnaise over the top and then sprinkle with the toasted sesame seeds. Pack half the rice on top, and then press down with the lid.

3 Lift off the sides of the sushi press, holding down the lid with your thumbs as you do so. Turn the sushi out onto a chopping board so that the layer of crab, avocado, and cucumber is on top. Slice into 5 equal pieces using a wet, very sharp knife. Wipe your knife on a damp cloth between cuts to keep your sushi bars neat. Repeat, to make 10 pieces in total.

4 Garnish the sushi with pickled ginger, and then arrange on a serving plate with the lemon slices and dill. Serve with wasabi paste and extra pickled ginger on the side.

ham & egg pressed sushi

ingredients

MAKES 10 PIECES

2–3 very thin slices of ham

1 tsp strong English mustard

½ quantity freshly cooked
   sushi rice (see page 8)

Japanese omelet

2 eggs

½ tsp superfine sugar

1 tsp mirin

½ tsp Japanese soy sauce

⅛ tsp salt

2 tsp vegetable oil

method

1 First make the omelet. Gently whisk the eggs with the sugar, mirin, soy sauce, and salt, taking care not to create large air bubbles. Strain into a pitcher.

2 Pour 1 tsp of the oil into a tamago pan or skillet, then heat over low-medium heat. Pour in the omelet mixture, tilting the pan to coat the bottom. When the omelet is almost set, flip it over and cook the other side. Turn the omelet out onto a plate lined with paper towels and let cool.

3 Wet the sushi mold. Cover the bottom with a layer of ham, trimming the slices so that there are no gaps, then smear with ½ tsp of the English mustard. Add a quarter of the sushi rice, and press down with the lid.

4 Add a layer of omelet, trimmed to fit the mold, then another quarter of the rice. Replace the lid and press down again.

5 Lift off the sides of the sushi mold, holding down the lid with your thumbs as you do so. Turn the sushi out onto a chopping board so that the ham is on top, and slice into 5 equal pieces using a wet, very sharp knife. Wipe your knife on a damp cloth between cuts to keep your sushi neat. Repeat, to make 10 pieces in total.

rare roast beef sushi balls with wasabi

ingredients

MAKES 10 PIECES

1 or 2 slices of rare roast beef

wasabi paste

¼ quantity freshly cooked
    sushi rice (see page 8)

1 tsp finely chopped scallion,
    green parts only, to
    garnish

Japanese soy sauce and
    pickled ginger, to serve

method

1 Cut the roast beef into 10 pieces measuring about 1 inch/2.5 cm square.

2 Cut a square of plastic wrap measuring 4 inch x 4 inch/10 cm x 10 cm. Lay a piece of roast beef in the center. Dab a little wasabi paste onto the beef.

3 Take 1½ tsp of sushi rice and gently roll into a ball. Lay it on top of the beef.

4 Wrap the plastic wrap around the rice and beef, twisting the 4 corners together to form a tight package so that the rice inside makes a smooth ball. Repeat to make 10 balls in total.

5 Unwrap the balls just before serving, and garnish with a little chopped scallion. Serve with soy sauce, pickled ginger, and extra wasabi paste alongside.

mediterranean pressed sushi

ingredients

MAKES 10 PIECES

2 red bell peppers, quartered
   and seeded

3½ oz/100 g mozzarella,
   cut into thin slices

handful of small basil leaves

4 sundried tomatoes in oil,
   drained and cut into strips

olive oil, for brushing

½ quantity freshly cooked
   sushi rice (see page 8)

method

1 Place the quartered bell peppers skin-side up under a hot broiler until the skin blackens. Let cool in a sealed plastic bag or box, peel off the skin, and cut the flesh into strips.

2 Wet the sushi mold to prevent the rice from sticking. Arrange the grilled bell pepper and mozzarella in wide, diagonal strips over the bottom of the sushi press, placing thinner strips of basil leaves and sundried tomatoes in-between. Brush with oil, then cover with half of the sushi rice. Press down with the lid.

3 Lift off the sides of the sushi mold, holding down the lid with your thumbs as you do so. Turn the sushi out onto a chopping board so that the layer of mozzarella and pepper is on top. Slice into 5 equal pieces using a wet, very sharp knife. Wipe your knife on a damp cloth between cuts to keep your sushi neat. Repeat, so that you have 10 pieces in total.

tofu sushi with ginger & scallion

ingredients

MAKES 10 PIECES

½ block firm tofu

½ sheet of toasted nori

½ quantity freshly cooked
   sushi rice (see page 8)

10 long chives, trimmed

1 tsp shredded gingerroot,
   pressed to remove excess
   water

method

1 Wrap the tofu in kitchen towels and place on a small chopping board. Place another chopping board on top to help squeeze out the excess water. Let stand for 30 minutes.

2 Cut the drained tofu into 10 slices about ¼ inch/5 mm thick, cutting crosswise across the block. Reserve any remaining tofu for another recipe. Cut the ½-sheet of nori into 10 strips about ½ inch/1 cm wide and 3 inch/7.5 cm long.

3 Wet a finger sushi mold. Fill each section with sushi rice, working the rice into the corners. Press down with the lid, remove it, and turn the neat blocks out onto a chopping board. Repeat so that you have 10 blocks.

4 Alternatively, shape the rice by hand. Take a golfball-sized amount of rice in the palm of one hand, then gently press it into an oblong, using your palm and the fingers of your other hand. The block should be 2 inch/5 cm long and ¾ inch/2 cm wide. Repeat to make 10 blocks, and place on a chopping board.

5 Lay a slice of tofu lengthwise across each rice block. Wrap a nori strip neatly around each one, tucking the ends under the rice block to secure. Knot a chive around each sushi to secure the tofu, and garnish with shredded ginger.

sweet rolled omelet sushi

ingredients

MAKES 10 PIECES

½ sheet of toasted nori
½ quantity freshly cooked
    sushi rice (see page 8)
Japanese soy sauce, pickled
    ginger, and wasabi paste,
    to serve

rolled omelet

6 eggs
1 tsp superfine sugar
2 tsp mirin
1 tsp Japanese soy sauce
¼ tsp salt
1-2 tsp vegetable oil

method

1 First make the omelet. Gently beat the eggs together with sugar, mirin, soy sauce, and salt, taking care not to create large air bubbles. Strain into a pitcher.

2 Heat a tamago pan or skillet over medium heat. Use a brush or folded piece of kitchen towel to oil the pan. Add a third of the egg mixture to the pan and tilt the pan to cover the bottom evenly. When the omelet has just set, fold it 4 times lengthwise towards you, using a wooden spatula. Set aside, trimming it into an oblong if you have used a round skillet.

3 Repeat with another third of the egg mixture, placing the first folded omelet on top of the omelet in the pan before you wrap it up. Do the same for the rest of the egg mixture, so that you end up with 1 thick roll. Let cool, then cut crosswise into 10 slices.

4 Cut the half-sheet of nori into 10 strips about ½ inch/1 cm wide and 3 inch/7.5 cm long.

5 Make 10 rice blocks using a finger sushi mold or by hand (see page 122) and place them on a chopping board.

6 Place a slice of rolled omelet onto each rice block. Wrap a nori strip neatly around each one, tucking the ends under the rice block to secure. Serve with soy sauce, pickled ginger, and wasabi paste.

asparagus & red bell pepper sushi

ingredients

MAKES 10 PIECES

2 red bell peppers, quartered
    and seeded
30 baby asparagus
½ sheet of toasted nori
½ quantity freshly cooked
    sushi rice (see page 8)
Japanese soy sauce, pickled
    ginger, and wasabi paste,
    to serve

method

1 Place the quartered bell peppers skin-side up under a hot broiler until the skin blackens. Let cool in a sealed plastic bag or box, peel off the skin, and cut the flesh into strips. Drop the asparagus into boiling water for 1–2 minutes to blanch, then dip into ice-cold water to stop the cooking.

2 Cut the half-sheet of nori into 10 strips about ½ inch/1 cm wide and 3 inch/7.5 cm long.

3 Wet a sushi mold to stop the rice from sticking. Arrange a layer of pepper strips over the bottom, leaving no gaps. Top with half of the sushi rice, and press down with the lid.

4 Lift off the sides of the sushi mold, holding down the lid with your thumbs as you do so. Turn the sushi out onto a chopping board so that the peppers are on top, and slice into 5 equal pieces using a wet, very sharp knife. Repeat, to make 10 pieces in total.

5 Place 3 asparagus tips lengthwise across the center of the pepper, and secure with a strip of nori, tucking the ends under the rice block to keep it neatly in place. Serve with soy sauce, pickled ginger, and wasabi paste.

spiced carrot sushi

ingredients

MAKES 10 PIECES

½ quantity freshly cooked
   sushi rice (see page 8)
10 long chives, trimmed
1 tsp shredded gingerroot,
   squeezed to remove
   excess water, to garnish
2 tsp finely chopped scallion,
   green parts only, to
   garnish
Japanese soy sauce, pickled
   ginger, and wasabi paste,
   to serve

spiced carrot

1 large carrot, peeled and cut
   into large thin slices
4 fl oz/125 ml/½ cup dashi
   stock (see page 194 or
   use instant granules)
2 tsp superfine sugar
2 tsp Japanese soy sauce

method

1 First prepare the spiced carrot. Put the dashi stock, sugar, and soy sauce into a small pan and set over low heat. Add the carrot slices and cook for 5–6 minutes, until tender but still retaining a little bite. Drain and let cool.

2 Wet the sushi mold to stop the rice from sticking. Cover the bottom with a layer of the spiced carrot. Top with half the sushi rice, then press down with the lid.

3 Lift off the sides of the sushi mold, holding down the lid with your thumbs as you do so. Turn the sushi out onto a chopping board so that the carrot layer is on top, and slice into 5 equal pieces. Repeat with the rest of the ingredients to make 10 pieces in total.

4 Top each sushi bar with a little shredded ginger and scallion. Serve with soy sauce, pickled ginger, and wasabi paste on the side.

fresh shiitake mushroom sushi

ingredients

MAKES 10 PIECES

1 tbsp Japanese soy sauce

10 fresh shiitake mushrooms, stems removed

½ sheet of toasted nori

½ quantity freshly cooked sushi rice (see page 8)

Japanese soy sauce, pickled ginger, and wasabi paste, to serve

method

1 Brush the soy sauce on the mushrooms, and cook under a hot broiler for 1–2 minutes on each side, or until tender.

2 Cut the half-sheet of nori into 10 strips about ½ inch/1 cm wide and 3 inch/7.5 cm long.

3 Wet a finger sushi mold. Fill each section with sushi rice, working the rice into the corners without pressing too hard. Press down with the lid, then remove it, and turn the neat blocks out onto a chopping board. Repeat so that you have 10 blocks.

4 Alternatively, shape the rice by hand. Take a golfball-sized amount of rice in the palm of one hand, then gently press it into an oblong, using your palm and the fingers of your other hand. The block should be 2 inch/5 cm long and ¾ inch/2 cm wide. Repeat to make 10 blocks, and place on a chopping board.

5 Place 1 grilled mushroom, skin-side down, on each rice block. Secure with a nori strip, tucking the ends under the rice block. Serve with soy sauce, pickled ginger, and wasabi paste on the side.

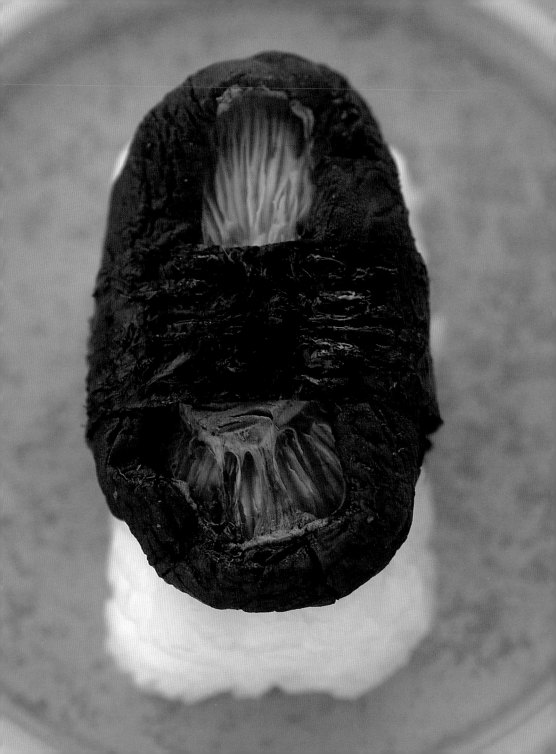

avocado sushi with tapenade

ingredients

MAKES 10 PIECES

½ sheet of toasted nori

½ quantity freshly cooked
    sushi rice (see page 8)

1 ripe avocado, pitted,
    peeled, and cut into thin
    slices

2 tsp tapenade

pickled ginger and wasabi
    paste, to serve

method

1 Cut the half-sheet of nori into 10 strips about ½ inch/1 cm wide and 3 inch/7.5 cm long.

2 Wet a finger sushi mold. Fill each section with sushi rice, working the rice into the corners without pressing too hard. Press down with the lid, then remove it, and turn the neat blocks out onto a chopping board. Repeat so that you have 10 blocks.

3 Alternatively, shape the rice by hand. Take a golfball-sized amount of rice in the palm of one hand, then gently press it into an oblong, using your palm and the fingers of your other hand. The block should be 2 inch/5 cm long and ¾ inch/2 cm wide. Repeat to make 10 blocks, and place on a chopping board.

4 Place a couple of slices of avocado lengthwise on each rice block. Secure with a nori strip, tucking the ends under the rice block. Put a dab of tapenade on the center of the nori strip. Serve with pickled ginger and wasabi paste alongside.

eggplant sushi with sweet soy sauce

ingredients

MAKES 10 PIECES

2 Japanese eggplants
olive oil, for brushing
½ quantity freshly cooked
   sushi rice (see page 8)
2 tsp white sesame seeds,
   toasted

sweet soy sauce

4 fl oz/125 ml/½ cup
   Japanese soy sauce
1½ tbsp superfine sugar
4 fl oz/125 ml/½ cup mirin

method

1 Cut the eggplants into ¼-inch/5-mm thick slices. They should be 1¾ inch wide and 3 inch/7.5 cm long so that they can be draped over the smaller rice blocks. Brush with a little olive oil and place under a medium-high grill for 6–8 minutes or until tender, turning once.

2 Place all the ingredients for the dipping sauce in a small pan, stir, and bring to a boil. Cook until reduced by half, then let cool.

3 Wet a finger sushi mold. Fill each section with sushi rice, working the rice into the corners without pressing too hard. Press down with the lid, then remove it, and turn the neat blocks out onto a chopping board. Repeat so that you have 10 blocks.

4 Alternatively, shape the rice by hand. Take a golfball-sized amount of rice in the palm of one hand, then gently press it into an oblong, using your palm and the fingers of your other hand. The block should be 2 inch/5 cm long and ¾ inch/2 cm wide. Repeat to make 10 blocks, and place on a chopping board.

5 Place one slice of eggplant on each rice block and scatter a few sesame seeds over the top. Serve with the sweet soy dipping sauce.

chirashi
sushi

Chirashi sushi is sushi in a bowl, the Japanese version of a rice salad. It is the easiest sushi to prepare, and it makes a great lunch dish. Chirashi is often called "housewife's sushi" because it is so commonly made at home in Japan. The base is freshly prepared sushi rice, which can be mixed with simple flavorings such as mushroom, ginger, or sesame seeds. The main ingredients are usually arranged on top, but you can also mix them in with rice—this type of sushi is called *gomoko zushi*.

As with all sushi, presentation is key. It is worth getting some pleasing wooden or lacquer Japanese bowls in which to serve your chirashi. You can also arrange all the ingredients in one large bowl and get everyone to help themselves, buffet-style. Fill your serving bowl or bowls to a depth of about two-thirds, then arrange the toppings attractively on top. You can add pickled ginger and wasabi paste to the bowl, or you can serve them alongside in bowls, with a small pitcher of soy sauce.

Because chirashi sushi is so easy to make, it is a good style to experiment with. You can use almost anything as a topping so long that its flavor marries well with the vinegared rice. The recipes that follow should give you some good ideas to start with, but feel free to mix and match as you please.

chirashi sushi with salmon

ingredients

SERVES 4

8 large raw shrimp, heads
  removed

salt

1 tbsp sake

1 tbsp rice vinegar

9 oz/250 g sashimi-grade
  salmon

3-inch/7.5-cm piece of
  kombu, cut into thin strips

juice of 1 lemon

4 oz/115 g green beans, tips
  removed

1 quantity freshly cooked
  sushi rice (see page 8)

2 oz/55 g lotus root, thinly
  sliced

4 tbsp salmon roe

4 shiso leaves, to garnish

Japanese soy sauce, pickled
  ginger, and wasabi paste,
  to serve

method

1 Insert a thin wooden skewer along the underside of each shrimp to prevent it from curling during cooking. Place 1 inch/2.5 cm of water in a large pan and add a little salt and the sake. Bring to a boil, add the skewered shrimp, and let simmer for 2 minutes or until they turn pink. Drain and let cool.

2 Peel each shrimp, cut along the back of the body, and scrape out the intestinal thread. Deepen the incision and carefully open the shrimp into a flat butterfly-shape. Sprinkle with the rice vinegar and place in the refrigerator until needed.

3 Slice the salmon into $1/3$-inch/8-mm thick strips, using a wet, very sharp knife and cutting across the grain. Wipe your knife on a damp cloth between each cut. Place in a bowl with the kombu strips and lemon juice. Let stand for 15 minutes, turning the fish once.

4 Drop the green beans into boiling salted water for 1 minute to blanch, then plunge into ice-cold water. Drain, then cut into strips.

5 Divide the sushi rice between 4 serving bowls. To each bowl, add a quarter of the salmon, 2 cooked shrimp, a quarter of the sliced green beans and lotus root, and 1 tbsp of the salmon roe. Garnish with a shiso leaf and serve with soy sauce, pickled ginger, and wasabi paste alongside.

chirashi sushi with smoked mackerel

ingredients

SERVES 4

8 snow peas

2-inch/5-cm piece of daikon
(long white radish)

1 quantity freshly cooked
sushi rice (see page 8)

juice and zest of 1 lemon

2 scallions, finely chopped

2 smoked mackerel, skin
removed and cut into
diagonal strips

½ English cucumber, peeled
and cut into slices

1 sheet of toasted nori, cut
into thin strips

4 tbsp pickled ginger

2 tsp wasabi paste

method

1 Drop the snow peas into boiling, salted water for 1 minute to blanch, then plunge into ice-cold water to stop the cooking. Drain well.

2 Shred the daikon using the finest setting on a mandolin or a very sharp knife. If you are using a knife, then cut the daikon into long, thin slices and cut each slice along its length as finely as you can. Rinse and then drain.

3 Mix the sushi rice with the lemon juice and lemon zest.

4 Divide the lemony rice between 4 serving bowls and sprinkle the scallion over the top. Arrange the mackerel, cucumber, snow peas, and daikon on top of the rice. Garnish with nori strips, and add 1 tbsp of pickled ginger and ½ tsp wasabi paste to each bowl.

marinated tuna chirashi sushi

ingredients

SERVES 4

12 oz/350 g sashimi-grade
    tuna
juice of 2 lemons
1 tbsp soy sauce
1 quantity freshly cooked
    sushi rice (see page 8)
4 tbsp finely chopped chives
4 tbsp pickled ginger
2 tsp wasabi paste
8 shiso leaves, to garnish
4 tsp white sesame seeds,
    toasted

method

1 Put the tuna into a bowl and pour the lemon juice and soy sauce over the top. Turn the tuna to coat, then place in the refrigerator and let marinate for 30 minutes.

2 Remove the tuna from the marinade and slice into $1/3$-inch/8-mm thick strips, using a wet, very sharp knife and cutting across the grain. Wipe your knife on a damp cloth between each cut to keep your tuna strips neat.

3 Divide the sushi rice between 4 serving bowls. Arrange the tuna slices on the rice and sprinkle the chives over the top. Add 1 tbsp pickled ginger and $1/2$ tsp wasabi paste to each bowl, garnish with a shiso leaf, and sprinkle with the toasted sesame seeds.

Thai-style chirashi sushi with crabmeat

ingredients

SERVES 4

6 oz/175 g cooked crabmeat

juice of 2 limes, plus 4 thin
    slices of lime to garnish

2 large red chiles, seeded
    and finely chopped

4 oz/115 g shelled fresh peas

salt

1 quantity freshly cooked
    sushi rice (see page 8)

2 tbsp chopped fresh cilantro

1 sheet of toasted nori, cut
    into thin strips

method

1 Put the crabmeat in a bowl and squeeze over the lime juice. Stir in the chopped chile.

2 Place the peas in a pan of boiling salted water for 2 minutes or until just-tender, then plunge into ice-cold water to stop the cooking. Drain well.

3 Add the peas to the sushi rice, turning the rice to mix evenly. Divide the mixture between 4 serving bowls.

4 Top each bowl with a quarter of the crab mixture and sprinkle with $1/2$ tbsp of the chopped cilantro. Add a quarter of the nori strips, and garnish with a slice of lime.

chirashi sushi with shrimp, crab & avocado

ingredients

SERVES 4

1 tbsp vegetable oil

6 large raw shrimp, shelled and deveined

1 cooked prepared crab

1 quantity freshly cooked sushi rice (see page 8)

juice and zest of 1 lemon

1 ripe avocado, stoned, peeled, and cut into strips

½ English cucumber, peeled and cut into slices

Japanese soy sauce, pickled ginger, and wasabi paste, to serve

method

1 Heat the oil in a skillet, then cook the shrimp by sautéing for 2 minutes on each side. Once they are cooked, let cool, then cut in half lengthwise. Lift the crabmeat out of the shell.

2 Mix the sushi rice with the lemon juice and lemon zest, then divide between 4 serving bowls. Arrange the cooked shrimp, crabmeat, and avocado and cucumber slices on top of the rice. Serve with soy sauce, pickled ginger, and wasabi paste.

chirashi sushi with lobster & wasabi mayonnaise

ingredients

SERVES 4

1 cooked prepared lobster

5 tbsp pickled ginger

1 quantity freshly cooked
    sushi rice (see page 8)

1/2 English cucumber, cut into
    slices

1 ripe avocado, peeled,
    pitted, and cut into slices

2 tsp wasabi paste

wasabi mayonnaise

2 tbsp Japanese mayonnaise

1 tsp wasabi paste, or to taste

method

1 Take the meat out of the lobster shell, keeping it in as large pieces as you can. If your lobster is whole, the best way to do this is to twist off the head and halve the body down the center with a big sharp knife or cleaver. The claws will have to be smashed open to get at the meat. Cover them with a cloth and hit them hard with a rolling pin.

2 Make the wasabi mayonnaise by mixing together the mayonnaise and wasabi. Chop 1 tbsp of the pickled ginger very finely and mix it with the sushi rice.

3 Divide the rice between 4 serving bowls. Arrange the lobster, cucumber, and avocado on top of the rice and spoon the wasabi mayonnaise into the gaps. Garnish each bowl with 1 tbsp of the pickled ginger and 1/2 tsp of the wasabi paste.

chirashi sushi on scallop shells

ingredients

MAKES 8 SHELLS

8 scallops with their shells
1 tbsp vegetable oil
zest and juice of $\frac{1}{2}$ lime
$\frac{1}{3}$ quantity freshly cooked
    sushi rice (see page 8)
small handful of fresh cilantro
    leaves
3 tbsp Japanese mayonnaise
pickled ginger and wasabi
    paste, to garnish

method

1 Remove the scallops from their shells. Clean the shells to use for serving.

2 Clean each scallop by pulling off the small, white shiny muscle and its membrane. Leave the roe attached, but snip off the black vein, if present, with a pair of kitchen scissors.

3 Heat the oil in a skillet and sauté the scallops for 2–3 minutes on each side, until they are lightly browned and cooked through. Squeeze a little lime juice over the scallops and let cool.

4 Mix the sushi rice with the remaining lime juice and zest.

5 Divide the lime-flavored sushi rice between the 8 scallop shells. Arrange a scallop along with a few cilantro leaves on top of the rice in each shell, then garnish with a piece of pickled ginger, a tiny amount of wasabi, and a heaping tsp of mayonnaise. Serve on a platter with a pile of chopsticks.

chirashi sushi with soy-glazed steak

ingredients

SERVES 4

8 dried shiitake mushrooms

2-inch/5-cm piece of daikon
(long white radish), peeled

2-inch/5-cm piece of carrot,
peeled

1 tbsp soy sauce

1 tsp mirin

1 tsp brown sugar

7 oz/200 g tenderloin steak,
trimmed

1 quantity freshly cooked
sushi rice (see page 8)

2 tsp wasabi paste

1 sheet of toasted nori, cut
into strips

pickled ginger, to serve

method

1 Soak the mushrooms in boiling water for 20 minutes, then simmer them in the same liquid for 3 minutes. Lift them out and squeeze them dry. Chop 4 mushrooms finely and halve the rest.

2 Shred the daikon and carrot using the finest setting on a mandolin or a very sharp knife. If you are using a knife, then cut the daikon and carrot into long, thin slices and cut each slice along its length as finely as you can. Rinse, drain, and refrigerate.

3 Preheat the broiler to its highest setting. Mix together the soy sauce, mirin, and brown sugar, then brush the mixture all over the steak. Broil the coated steak for 3 minutes on each side. Let it rest for a minute, then cut into strips.

4 Mix the sushi rice with the chopped shiitake mushrooms. Divide the mushroom rice between 4 serving bowls and arrange the broiled steak and halved mushrooms on top. Add a neat pile of shredded daikon and carrot to each bowl, together with $1/2$ tsp of the wasabi. Garnish each bowl with nori strips, and serve with pickled ginger on the side.

chirashi sushi with teriyaki chicken

ingredients

SERVES 4

4 skinless, boneless chicken
    breasts, weighing about
    5½ oz/150 g each
1 tbsp vegetable oil
1 quantity freshly cooked
    sushi rice (see page 8)
finely chopped scallion, green
    parts only, and sticks of
    cucumber, to garnish
sweet chili sauce, to serve

teriyaki marinade

4 tbsp Japanese soy sauce
2 tbsp mirin
2 tbsp sake
2 tsp superfine sugar
1 tsp shredded gingerroot
    (optional)
1 garlic clove, crushed
    (optional)

method

1 Combine all the ingredients for the marinade in a bowl that is large enough to take the chicken as well. Add the chicken and turn to coat. Cover and let marinate in the refrigerator for 30 minutes.

2 Heat the oil in a skillet. Remove the chicken from the marinade, add to the skillet, and cook for 4 minutes. Turn over, brush with marinade, and cook for another 4–6 minutes, or until the chicken is tender and the juices run clear when a skewer is inserted into the thickest part of the meat. Once you have brushed on the marinade, do not add on any more during the cooking process.

3 Transfer the cooked chicken to a chopping board and cut into thin diagonal slices, holding your knife at a 45° angle to the board.

4 Divide the rice between 4 serving bowls. Top with the sliced chicken and garnish with chopped scallion and cucumber sticks. Serve with the sweet chili sauce.

sesame-tofu chirashi sushi

ingredients

SERVES 4

1 block firm tofu

1 quantity freshly cooked
   sushi rice (see page 8)

2 red bell peppers, quartered
   and seeded

1 sheet of toasted nori

4 tbsp pickled ginger

2 tsp wasabi paste

2 tbsp finely chopped
   scallions, green parts only,
   to garnish

pickled ginger and wasabi
   paste, to serve

sesame marinade

¼ tsp sesame oil

1 garlic clove, crushed

¾-inch/2-cm piece
   gingerroot, peeled and
   shredded

3 tbsp Japanese soy sauce

4 tbsp sake

1 tsp dark brown sugar

1 tsp red chili flakes

method

1 Wrap the tofu in kitchen towels and place on a small chopping board. Put another chopping board on top and let stand for 30 minutes to squeeze out the excess water. Then cut the tofu into slices about ⅓ inch/8 mm thick, cutting crosswise across the block. Transfer the tofu slices to a small bowl.

2 Place all the ingredients for the marinade into a bowl or pitcher, and stir until the sugar dissolves. Pour the marinade over the tofu slices and carefully turn to coat. Place in the refrigerator for 20 minutes to marinate.

3 Put the quartered bell peppers skin-side up under a hot broiler until the skin blackens. Let cool in a sealed plastic bag or box, then peel off the skin and cut the flesh into strips.

4 Cut the nori sheet into squares measuring about ½ inch x ½ inch/1 cm x 1 cm.

5 Divide the sushi rice between 4 serving bowls. Arrange the tofu slices on the rice and spoon a little of the marinade on top. Add a quarter of the pepper strips to each bowl, along with a few nori squares, 1 tbsp pickled ginger, and ½ tsp wasabi paste. Garnish with the chopped scallions, and serve with pickled ginger and wasabi paste.

oyster mushroom & fried tofu chirashi sushi

ingredients

SERVES 4

2 sheets of abura-age (deep-fried tofu)

18 fl oz/500 ml/2 cups dashi stock (see page 194 or use instant granules)

4 tbsp sake

2 tbsp sugar

4 tbsp Japanese soy sauce

2 tbsp vegetable oil

1 lb/500 g fresh oyster or shiitake mushrooms, thinly sliced

1 quantity freshly cooked sushi rice (see page 8)

2 tsp white sesame seeds, toasted

Japanese soy sauce, pickled ginger, and wasabi paste, to serve

method

1 Cut the fried tofu sheets into thin strips. Place the dashi stock, sake, sugar, and the soy sauce in a pan, stir, then add the tofu strips. Cook over low heat for 15 minutes, uncovered, until the liquid has reduced by half. Drain well.

2 Heat the oil in a skillet. Add the mushrooms and cook, stirring, over medium-high heat for 2 minutes, until soft.

3 Divide the rice between 4 serving bowls. Top with the seasoned fried tofu and the cooked mushrooms, and sprinkle with the toasted sesame seeds. Serve with soy sauce, pickled ginger, and wasabi paste alongside.

chirashi sushi with feta & sunblush tomatoes

ingredients

SERVES 4

6 oz/175 g feta cheese

3 oz/85 g sunblush tomatoes
in oil

handful of basil leaves,
shredded, plus a few
whole leaves to garnish

1 quantity freshly cooked
sushi rice (see page 8)

2 oz/55 g of baby spinach
greens

method

1 Drain the feta and cut it into small cubes. Slice the sunblush tomatoes into thin strips and pat with kitchen towels to remove any excess oil. Mix carefully into the feta with the shredded basil.

2 Divide the sushi rice between 4 serving bowls. Arrange a quarter of the baby spinach greens on each serving, and top with a mound of the feta and tomato mixture. Garnish each serving with a couple of whole basil leaves.

chirashi sushi with omelet, asparagus & mushroom

ingredients

SERVES 4

16 thin asparagus spears

12 snow peas

1 quantity freshly cooked
sushi rice (see page 8)

1 English cucumber,
seeded and cut into thin
2-inch/5-cm long sticks

1 sheet of nori, cut into
shreds

4 tbsp pickled ginger

2 tsp wasabi

spiced mushrooms

1 oz/25 g dried shiitake
mushrooms

6 fl oz/175 ml/¾ cup dashi
stock (see page 194 or
use instant granules)

1 tbsp mirin

Japanese omelet

3 eggs

½ tsp superfine sugar

1 tsp mirin

½ tsp Japanese soy sauce

⅛ tsp salt

2 tsp vegetable oil

method

1 First prepare the spiced mushrooms. Soak the mushrooms in hot water for 30 minutes. Cut them into thin slices, discard the stems, and place in a pan with the dashi stock. Simmer for 15 minutes, take off the heat, and stir in the mirin. Let cool, then drain well.

2 Make the omelet mixture: gently whisk the eggs with the sugar, mirin, soy sauce, and salt, taking care not to create large air bubbles. Strain into a pitcher.

3 Pour 1 tsp of the oil into a tamago pan or skillet, then heat over low-medium heat. Pour in half of the omelet mixture, tilting the pan to coat the base. When the omelet is almost set, flip it over and cook the other side. Turn out onto a plate lined with paper towels and let cool. Repeat to make another omelet. Cut the omelets into fine shreds and set aside.

4 Place the asparagus spears and snow peas in boiling water for 1–2 minutes to blanch. Remove and plunge into ice-cold water.

5 Divide the sushi rice between serving bowls. Top with a quarter of the spiced mushroom slices and cucumber sticks, 4 asparagus spears, and 3 snow peas. Sprinkle with the omelet shreds and nori. Add 1 tbsp pickled ginger and ½ tsp wasabi paste to each bowl.

green bean & tomato chirashi sushi

ingredients

SERVES 4

5 oz/140 g very thin green
    beans
5 oz/140 g tomatoes on the
    vine
1 yellow bell pepper
1 quantity freshly cooked
    sushi rice (see page 8)
4 tsp white sesame seeds,
    toasted
Japanese soy sauce, pickled
    ginger, and wasabi paste,
    to serve

method

1 Drop the beans into a pan of boiling water for 1–2 minutes to blanch. Plunge into ice-cold water to stop the cooking, then drain.

2 Cut the tomatoes into thin slices, discarding the seeds.

3 Cut the bell pepper into quarters, remove and discard the seeds, and cut into thin strips.

4 Divide the sushi rice between 4 serving bowls. Arrange the blanched green beans, sliced tomatoes, and pepper strips on the rice. Scatter the toasted sesame seeds over the top. Serve with soy sauce, pickled ginger, and wasabi paste alongside.

accompaniments & desserts

Japanese cuisine does not involve complicated sauces and garnishes. The only things you need serve alongside your sushi are soy sauce, pickled ginger, and wasabi paste. But one or two other dishes will help to make your meal more substantial. The Japanese often drink a clear soup at the start of a sushi meal, and miso soup at the end. You can follow this custom, or you can simply serve soup with your sushi—perhaps with a simple green salad or a few blanched soybeans too.

If you have time, you may also want to add a hot dish or two to the meal. Seafood and vegetarian tempura are extremely popular in Japan and abroad, as are the delicious little appetizers known as gyoza—pork dumplings. Pickles are available ready-made from specialist shops, but if you have time, it is worth making some of your own—pickled ginger, for example, is very tasty, and will keep for several weeks in the refrigerator. A homemade dipping sauce is a good way of introducing some different flavors.

To finish your meal, a selection of fresh fruit, neatly cut and beautifully presented on a platter, is ideal. For something more adventurous you can try Japanese-style ice cream. Hot green tea or sake served at room temperature are the traditional drinks to have with sushi, but a crisp lager or white wine also go well.

dashi stock with tofu and chives

ingredients

SERVES 4

1¾ pints/1 liter/4 cups water

3-inch/7.5-cm square piece
    kombu (sun-dried kelp)

½ oz/15 g dried bonito fish
    flakes

1 tbsp sake

1 tbsp Japanese soy sauce

salt

3 oz/85 g firm tofu, cut into
    small cubes

small handful of chives, cut
    into 1-inch/2.5-cm lengths

method

1 Put the water into a pan. Cut a few slits along one edge of the kombu to help release the flavor and add to the water. Bring to a boil, and then remove the kombu.

2 Add the bonito flakes and take the pan off the heat straight away. Line a strainer with muslin and pour the stock through it. Stir in the sake, soy sauce, and salt to taste.

3 Arrange the tofu cubes and chopped chives in 4 serving bowls, then pour the dashi stock over the top. Serve immediately.

dashi stock with red snapper

ingredients

SERVES 4

5½ oz/150 g red snapper fillets

1 quantity dashi stock (see page 194)

small handful of chives, cut into 1-inch/2.5-cm lengths

method

1 Cut the fish into 8 equal pieces.

2 Heat the dashi stock through, then add the fish to the pan. Bring the stock to a boil and then take off the heat straightaway. Let the fish cook in the hot stock.

3 Using a slotted spoon, transfer 2 pieces of fish to each serving bowl. Pour the stock over the top and garnish with the chives.

miso soup

ingredients

SERVES 4

1 quantity dashi stock (see page 194)

6 oz/175 g firm tofu, cut into ½-inch/1-cm cubes

4 shiitake or white mushrooms, sliced

4 tbsp miso paste

2 scallions, finely sliced

2 tsp white sesame seeds, toasted

method

1 Put the dashi stock into a pan and heat through. Add the cubed tofu and sliced mushrooms, and let simmer gently for 3 minutes. Add the miso and stir until it has dissolved completely.

2 Turn off the heat, add the scallions, and divide the soup between 4 serving bowls. Scatter ½ tsp of the toasted sesame seeds over each serving.

vegetable & tofu tempura

ingredients

SERVES 4

5½ oz/150 g package
  tempura mix
1 potato, peeled and cut into
  ½-inch/1-cm thick pieces
¼ butternut squash, peeled
  and cut into ½-inch/1-cm
  thick pieces
1 small sweet potato, peeled
  and cut into ½-inch/1-cm
  thick pieces
1 small eggplant, cut into
  ½-inch/1-cm thick pieces
6 green beans, trimmed
1 red bell pepper, seeded and
  cut into thick strips
6 whole shiitake or white
  mushrooms, stalks
  removed
1 stalk broccoli, broken
  into florets
12 oz/350 g firm tofu, cubed
vegetable oil, for deep-frying
sweet chili sauce or tempura
  dipping sauce (see page
  204), to serve

method

1 Blend the tempura mix with the amount of water described on the package instructions until you have a lumpy batter full of air bubbles. Do not try to make the batter smooth or it will be too heavy.

2 Coat all the prepared vegetables and cubed tofu in the batter.

3 Add the oil to a deep-fryer and heat to 350–375°F/180–190°C, or until a cube of bread browns in 30 seconds.

4 Put the battered vegetables into the oil 3 at a time. If you add too many pieces at one time the oil temperature will drop and the batter will be soggy. Cook for 2–3 minutes, until the batter turns a light golden color. Remove and drain on paper towels to blot up the excess oil.

5 Serve hot, with the sweet chili sauce or tempura dipping sauce on the side.

seafood tempura

ingredients

SERVES 4

8 large raw shrimp, shelled
   and deveined

8 squid rings

5½ oz/150 g package
   tempura mix

4 scallops, without corals,
   cleaned

7 oz/200 g firm white fish
   fillets, cut into strips

vegetable oil, for deep-frying

Japanese soy sauce or
   tempura dipping sauce
   (see page 204), to serve

method

1 Make little cuts on the underside of the shrimp to keep them straight while they cook. Pull any membranes off the squid rings.

2 Blend the tempura mix with the amount of water described on the package instructions until you have a lumpy batter full of air bubbles. Do not try to make the batter smooth or it will be too heavy.

3 Coat all the prepared seafood in the batter.

4 Add the oil to a deep-fryer and heat to 350–375°F/180–190°C, or until a cube of bread browns in 30 seconds.

5 Add the battered seafood pieces 3 at a time. If you add too many pieces at one time the oil temperature will drop and the batter will be soggy. Cook for 2–3 minutes, until the batter turns a light golden color. Remove and drain on paper towels to blot up the excess oil.

6 Serve hot, with the soy sauce or tempura dipping sauce on the side.

tempura dipping sauce

ingredients

SERVES 4

4 tbsp dashi stock (see page 194 or use instant granules)

4 tsp mirin

2 tbsp Japanese soy sauce

method

1 Place the dashi stock in a small bowl. If using instant granules, add a large pinch to 4 tbsp boiling water and stir until dissolved.

2 Add the mirin and soy sauce, and stir to mix. Serve with seafood or vegetable tempura.

gyoza

ingredients

MAKES 24 PIECES

24 gyoza wonton skins

vegetable oil, for frying

pork filling

3½ oz/100 g white cabbage, finely shredded

2 scallions, very finely chopped

6 oz/175 g/¾ cup fresh ground pork

½-inch/1-cm piece fresh gingerroot, finely shredded

2 garlic cloves, crushed

1 tbsp Japanese soy sauce

2 tsp mirin

pinch of white pepper

salt

soy dipping sauce

2 tbsp rice vinegar

2 tbsp Japanese soy sauce

splash of water

method

1 To make the filling, mix all the ingredients together in a bowl. Season to taste with salt.

2 Lay a gyoza wonton skin flat on the palm of your hand and put 1 heaping tsp of the filling in the center. Brush a little water around the edges of the wonton skin. Fold up the skin sides to meet in a ridge along the center and press the edges together. Brush the curved edges of the skin with a little more water and make a series of little folds along the edges. Repeat with the remaining wonton skins and filling to make 24 pieces in total.

3 Heat a little oil in a lidded skillet and add as many gyoza as will fit in the bottom of the skillet with just a little space between them. Cook for 2 minutes, or until the undersides are browned.

4 Add water to a depth of about ⅛ inch/3 mm, cover the pan, and let simmer over low heat for 6 minutes or until the skins are translucent and cooked. Uncover the skillet and increase the heat to bubble away any excess water. Remove from the skillet and keep warm while you cook the remaining gyoza.

4 Place the ingredients for the soy dipping sauce in a small bowl and stir to combine. Serve with the gyoza.

yakitori chicken

ingredients

MAKES 6 SKEWERS

4 skinless, boneless chicken
thighs or 2 chicken
breasts, about 14 oz/400 g
total weight, cut into
24 chunks
4 scallions, cut into
18 short lengths

yakitori marinade

6 tbsp Japanese soy sauce
6 tbsp mirin
4 tbsp sake
2 tbsp superfine sugar

method

1 Soak 6 short wooden skewers in water for at least 20 minutes to prevent burning.

2 Meanwhile, make the marinade. Put the soy sauce, mirin, sake, and sugar into a small pan and bring to a boil. Reduce the heat and let simmer for 1 minute, then remove from the heat and let cool. Reserve a little of the sauce for drizzling over the skewers.

3 Preheat the broiler to high. Thread 4 pieces of chicken and 3 pieces of scallion onto each skewer, then brush the skewers with the sauce. Cook under the broiler for 4 minutes, then turn over and brush with more sauce mixture. Cook for an additional 4 minutes, or until the chicken is cooked through.

4 Serve the skewers drizzled with the reserved soy sauce mixture.

seasoned tofu

ingredients

SERVES 2

10½ oz/300 g silken tofu,
   drained
4 tbsp vegetable oil
2 scallions, finely sliced
½ fresh red chile,
   finely sliced
1 tbsp Japanese soy sauce
1 tsp sesame oil

method

1 Place the tofu on a heatproof serving plate. Cut the block into cubes, but keep it intact.

2 Heat the oil in a small pan over high heat until hot. Add the sliced scallions and chile and wait until they begin to sizzle.

3 Pour the hot oil mixture over the tofu, then sprinkle with the soy sauce and sesame oil. Serve as a block.

edamame

ingredients

SERVES 4

1 lb 2 oz/500 g frozen
   soybeans, in their pods
sea salt flakes

method

1 Bring a large pan of water to a boil. Add the beans and cook for 3 minutes, or until tender.

2 Drain well, sprinkle with salt flakes to taste, and toss together. Serve warm or cold.

seaweed salad

ingredients

SERVES 4

¾ oz/20 g assorted dried
    seaweed, such as
    wakame, hijiki, and arame
1 English cucumber
2 scallions, shredded
1 box of mustard and cress,
    snipped

sesame dressing

2 tbsp rice vinegar
2 tsp Japanese soy sauce
1 tbsp mirin
2 tsp sesame oil
1 tsp white miso

method

1 Soak the different seaweeds in separate bowls of cold water—the wakame will need 10 minutes and the others 30 minutes. Drain.

2 Cook the wakame only in a pan of boiling water for 2 minutes, then drain and let cool. Put all the seaweeds in a serving bowl.

3 Halve the cucumber lengthwise. Reserve half for another recipe, scoop the seeds out of the remaining half, and finely slice the flesh. Add to the seaweeds with the chopped scallions and the snipped mustard and cress.

4 Place all the ingredients for the dressing in a small pitcher and stir to combine. Add to the bowl, and toss the salad before serving.

daikon & cucumber salad

ingredients

SERVES 4

8-inch/20-cm piece of daikon
(long white radish)
1 English cucumber
handful of baby spinach
greens, chopped
3 red radishes, sliced into
thin rounds
a few leaves of Chinese
cabbage, cut into thin
strips
1 tbsp sunflower seeds
2 tsp white sesame seeds,
toasted

wasabi dressing

4 tbsp rice vinegar
2 tbsp grapeseed oil
1 tsp light soy sauce
1 tsp wasabi paste
½ tsp sugar
salt, to taste

method

1 Shred the daikon using the finest setting on a mandolin or a very sharp knife. If you are using a knife, then cut the daikon into long, thin slices and cut each slice along its length as finely as you can. Rinse under cold water, then drain well.

2 Halve the cucumber lengthwise, reserve half for another recipe, and use a teaspoon to scoop the seeds out of the remaining half. Peel and slice in the same way as the daikon.

3 Place the sliced daikon and cucumber in a salad bowl with the chopped spinach greens. Add the sliced radishes and Chinese cabbage.

4 Place the ingredients for the dressing in a small pitcher and stir to mix. Pour the dressing over the salad, toss gently to mix, and sprinkle with the sunflower seeds and the toasted sesame seeds.

green beans with sesame dressing

ingredients

SERVES 4

7 oz/200 g green beans
pinch of salt
1 tbsp sesame paste
1 tsp superfine sugar
1 tsp miso paste
2 tsp Japanese soy sauce

method

1 Cook the beans in a pan of simmering water for 4–5 minutes, until tender. Remove from the heat and drain.

2 Mix the remaining ingredients to a paste in a bowl that is large enough to take the beans. Toss the beans in the paste, then let cool before serving.

homemade pickled ginger

ingredients

**MAKES 4 OZ/115 G/
1 CUP**

3½ oz/100 g fresh gingerroot

1 tsp salt

4 fl oz/125 ml/½ cup rice
    vinegar

2 tbsp superfine sugar

4 tbsp water

method

1 Peel the ginger. Use a mandolin or vegetable peeler to slice it into long thin slivers, cutting along the grain. Sprinkle the slices with the salt, cover, and let stand for 30 minutes.

2 Place the salted ginger in boiling water for 30 seconds to blanch. Drain well.

3 Put the rice vinegar, sugar, and water into a small bowl. Stir to dissolve the sugar.

4 Place the ginger slices in a bowl, pour over the rice vinegar mixture, and turn to coat. Cover and let marinate for at least 24 hours in the refrigerator (it will turn slightly pink). Pickled ginger will keep for several weeks if stored in a sterile airtight container in the refrigerator.

pickled daikon & carrot

ingredients

SERVES 4

4-inch/10-cm daikon (long white radish), peeled

1 carrot, peeled

½ tsp salt

1 tbsp sugar

2 tbsp rice vinegar

1 tsp white sesame seeds, toasted

method

1 Use a mandolin or vegetable peeler to slice the daikon and carrot into long thin slivers. Sprinkle the slices with the salt, cover, and let stand for 30 minutes. Place in a strainer and gently press to extract the water.

2 Put the sugar and rice vinegar into a bowl that is large enough to take the daikon and carrot. Stir until the sugar has dissolved.

3 Add the daikon and carrot, and toss to coat. Refrigerate for 8 hours or overnight. Sprinkle with the toasted sesame seeds before serving.

pickled cucumber

ingredients

SERVES 4

½ English cucumber

1⅛ tsp salt

1 tbsp rice vinegar

1 tsp sugar

method

1 Slice the cucumber into thin rounds. Place the slices in a shallow bowl and sprinkle with 1 tsp of the salt. Leave to stand for 5 minutes.

2 Rinse the cucumber slices under running water, then drain well.

3 Place the remaining ⅛ tsp salt, rice vinegar, and sugar in a bowl that is large enough to take the cucumber, and stir to mix. Add the cucumber slices and toss to coat. Refrigerate for 8 hours or overnight.

ginger & sesame dipping sauce

ingredients

**MAKES 4 FL OZ/
125 ML/½ CUP**

1½-inch/4-cm piece very
    fresh gingerroot
4 tbsp Japanese soy sauce
2 tbsp mirin
2 tbsp sake
¼ tsp sesame oil
1 tsp rice vinegar

method

1 Shred the gingerroot into a small bowl and then press the flesh with the back of a teaspoon. Pour off 1 tsp fresh ginger juice and discard the pulp.

2 Place the ginger juice in a small bowl, add the soy sauce, mirin, sake, sesame oil, and rice vinegar, and stir to combine. Serve straight away or keep in a sealed container in the refrigerator for up to a week.

ponzu dipping sauce

ingredients

**MAKES 4 FL OZ/
125 ML/½ CUP**

2 tbsp mirin

1½ tbsp rice vinegar

2 tsp light soy sauce

1½ tbsp bonito flakes

3 tbsp fresh lemon juice

method

1 Place all the ingredients in a small pan and bring to a boil. Remove from the heat and let cool before serving as a dipping sauce.

teriyaki dipping sauce

ingredients

**MAKES 4 FL OZ/
125 ML/½ CUP**

4 tbsp Japanese soy sauce

2 tbsp mirin

2 tbsp sake

2 tsp superfine sugar

1 tsp shredded gingerroot
(optional)

1 garlic clove, crushed
(optional)

method

1 Place the soy sauce, mirin, sake, and sugar in a small pan with the shredded ginger and crushed garlic, if using.

2 Set over low heat and stir until the sugar has dissolved. Heat for 15 minutes or until the sauce has thickened. Let cool before serving.

japanese oranges

ingredients

SERVES 4

4 large oranges

1½ tbsp superfine sugar

8 fl oz/250 ml/1 cup
   Japanese plum wine

method

1 Cut the top and bottom off each orange using a small serrated knife. Working over a bowl so that you can catch the juices, cut away the peel and pith, following the curve of the fruit. Now cut between the membranes to release the orange segments, placing each one in the bowl as you go. Squeeze the membranes over the bowl to extract any remaining juice before discarding them.

2 Add the sugar to the wine and stir until the sugar dissolves. Pour the sweetened wine over the prepared oranges and refrigerate for 30 minutes before serving.

green tea ice cream

ingredients

SERVES 4

7 fl oz/200 ml/scant 1 cup
   milk
2 egg yolks
2 tbsp superfine sugar
2 tbsp maccha green
   tea powder
3½ fl oz/100 ml/generous
   ⅓ cup hot water
7 fl oz/200 ml/scant 1 cup
   heavy cream, lightly
   whipped

method

1 Pour the milk into a pan and heat to boiling point. Meanwhile, whisk the egg yolks with the sugar in a heatproof bowl.

2 Pour the milk onto the egg mixture, stirring constantly, then pour all the mixture back into the pan and stir well.

3 Cook over low heat, stirring constantly, for 3 minutes, or until the mixture is thick enough to coat the back of a spoon. Remove from the heat and let cool.

4 Mix the green tea powder with the hot water in a pitcher, pour into the cooled custard, and mix well. Fold in the whipped cream.

5 Transfer to an ice-cream maker and freeze according to the manufacturer's instructions. Alternatively, transfer to a freezerproof container and freeze for 2 hours. Turn into a bowl and beat with a fork to break down the ice crystals, then return to the freezerproof container and freeze for an additional 2 hours. Beat again, then return to the freezer and freeze overnight, or until solid.

mango squares

ingredients

SERVES 4

20 fl oz/625 ml/scant
   2½ cups mango juice

1½ tbsp agar powder
   or flakes

4 fl oz/125 ml/½ cup
   hot water

peanut oil, for brushing
   (optional)

method

1 Put the mango juice in a heatproof bowl.

2 Place the agar in a pan with the water and bring to a simmer. Let simmer gently for 2–3 minutes, then pour into the mango juice and mix well.

3 Brush a shallow, rectangular pan with the oil, or line with plastic wrap. Pour in the mango mixture, cover with plastic wrap, and let chill for 4 hours, or until set. Cut into cubes or diamond shapes to serve.

lychee sherbert

ingredients

SERVES 4

14 oz/400 g canned lychees,
   drained, or 1 lb/450 g
   fresh lychees, peeled and
   pitted

2 tbsp confectioners' sugar

1 egg white

1 lemon, thinly sliced,
   to decorate

method

1 Put the lychee flesh into a blender or food processor with the sugar. Blend to a purée.

2 Press the lychee purée through a strainer to remove any remaining solid pieces, transfer to a freezerproof container, and freeze for 3 hours.

3 Turn the mixture into the blender or food processor and blend until slushy. Keeping the motor running, add the egg white, then return the mixture to the freezerproof container and freeze for 8 hours or overnight. Decorate with lemon slices before serving.